119

Dr. G. W. Peters

The Kingship of Christ

AN INTERPRETATION OF RECENT EUROPEAN THEOLOGY

The Kingship of Christ

AN INTERPRETATION OF RECENT EUROPEAN THEOLOGY

THE STONE LECTURES FOR 1947
DELIVERED AT PRINCETON THEOLOGICAL SEMINARY

by

W. A. Visser 't Hooft, D.D.

HARPER & BROTHERS   NEW YORK & LONDON

THE KINGSHIP OF CHRIST

CONTENTS

It is nearly half a century ago that the great Dutch theologian and statesman, Dr. Abraham Kuyper, opened his Stone Lectures on Calvinism with the remark that, compared to the foaming waters of the stream of life in America, life in Europe seemed to be slow-moving and even frozen. These words help us to measure the distance which we have traveled since. The American current is still running swiftly. But the European stream is no longer frozen. In Europe the thaw has set in, the ice has been broken and the torrents are causing serious inundations. Fifty years of war, of social disintegration, of totalitarian nihilism have shaken the Old World. So much so, that it is as yet impossible to arrive at a clear diagnosis of the new situation. If we have learned anything in Europe during these years, it is that the only safe statement about the future is that we know nothing about it. That is why the judgment that Europe is finished does not depress us and the statement that out of suffering and chaos a new Europe is arising does not impress us.

But in that wild, unpredictable Europe there is a Church of Christ. It has long ceased to be the dominating factor of European life. It represents in many countries a small minority surrounded by paganized masses. It has greatly suffered in its outward life. Its leadership is inadequate in numbers and very tired of the exertions of recent years. It does not meet with a very remarkable response from the postwar generation. But it is by no means dying. On the contrary. It goes through a crisis of renewal. Within it new forces are in conflict with old forces. It has not for nothing found itself suddenly in the center of the great battle for Europe's soul. The creative astonishment about the mission with which it was entrusted in recent years has not produced that total reconstruction of life for which many were longing, but it is still at work in it. The healthy shock which came when it realized its own guilt in the European tragedy has not led it yet to a sufficiently deep repentance, but it has led to a new concern with its task in the world. And, most important of all and underlying it all, the Word of God is taking hold of it, overcomes its confusion and uncertainty and gathers the Church anew.

A European Christian who has the privilege of speaking to American fellow Christians today must try to throw light on the meaning of this new era in

European Church history. It is not necessary to speak about the outward developments, for these have been interpreted quite fully in the many books and articles which have been devoted to the struggle of the churches in the war years and to their difficulties in the postwar years. But it is necessary to dwell on the deeper currents of thought and life which manifest themselves in European churches. What lessons have they learned? What new insights have been given to them? What creative theological developments have taken place?

My purpose is, therefore, not to give a general survey of all trends of thought in European Continental Christianity but to describe those developments in the Reformation churches which represent their response to the questions of life and death which they have had to face in the critical years and still face today.

Such an undertaking is, of course, full of risks. It cannot and should not be done from the point of view of the spectator but from that of the churchman who has his own specific standpoint. It reflects a personal choice. Many of my European colleagues would interpret the situation differently or will feel that I am doing less than justice to important aspects of thought and life in European Protestantism. I believe, however, that the risk is worth taking. For it is only through such attempts, however imperfect, at the drawing of conclusions from the events of recent years that we can come to an ecumenical conversation among the churches in different parts of the world.

It follows from what has been said that these lectures do not claim to present original thought. Quite apart from the fact that a servant of the World Council of Churches is unable to give as much time to theological study as he would like to do, I believe that the ecumenical situation today demands simple expositions of whatever consensus has been reached or may be expected, rather than further additions to the already undigestible mass of individual theological contributions. The use which I have made of the work of many others should be considered as an expression of gratitude for all that I have learned from them.

I do not think for a moment that the convictions which I will present are exclusively held in the European churches. It would not have been difficult to quote the theologians of many other churches whose contributions point in the same direction and to the same conclusions. If I have deliberately confined myself to Continental European thought and life, this is because I want to describe the specific movement which has taken place in one part of the world as a result of the interaction of theology and events in the life of Church and world.

My hope is that these lectures may serve especially as a contribution to that transoceanic ecumenical conversation between the American and the European churches which needs so badly to be resumed. The European churches are deeply grateful for the astonishingly generous help which has come to them from their American sister churches. They begin to realize that they are shamefully ignorant about the life of the American churches. And they are more deeply interested in an exchange of thought and life with American Christianity than they have ever been.

What should be the central theme of this interchurch conversation? At a time when many American Christians realize the need for a restatement of the social gospel of the twenties and when the European churches are at last beginning to discover their responsibility to the world, it would seem that that main theme is: the nature of Christ's Kingship and its implications for the Church and the world.

In our day and generation the Church has the specific mission to get beyond the sterile alternative of a social gospel which is not really a gospel but a system of moral laws and an individualistic orthodoxy which is not really orthodox, since it does not have the cosmic, world-embracing outlook of the Bible. Only if we can get rid of both the old-style moralism and the old-style pietism is there any hope that the Church will speak once again to the condition of man in the modern world.

I believe that slowly but surely the road to a restatement of the Gospel of the God who reconciles the world to Himself in Christ is being opened up. We are only at the beginning of that road and I do not for a moment pretend that I am able to lead my readers to its end. But even so, it is more than worth while to try to show a direction in which we might travel farther and, if God wills, travel together.

W. A. VISSER 'T HOOFT

April, 1947
Geneva, Switzerland

The Kingship of Christ

AN INTERPRETATION OF RECENT EUROPEAN THEOLOGY

CHAPTER I

The Kingship of Christ in Protestant Theology

The Church preaches "the unsearchable riches of Christ" (Ephesians 3:8). It knows that it will never express fully and adequately what God in Christ has done for mankind. But precisely because it realizes its own impotence to do justice to the plenitude of the Gospel, it seeks to bring a certain order in the wealth which that Gospel contains. This ordering which is the proper task of theology is never an aim in itself but an indispensable preparation for, and testing of, the witness which the Church renders.

The doctrine of the threefold office of Christ is a

typical example of such pastoral dogmatics. Its purpose is not only to reinterpret the Biblical message in its comprehensiveness and in its diversity but also to provide a basis and norm for the true proclamation of Jesus Christ. It is, therefore, not a speculative but a practical doctrine. Calvin, who has been the first to give it a central place in dogmatics (1) and to elaborate its implications, explains its *raison d'être* as follows: "*Afin que la foy trouve en Jésus Christ ferme matière de salut pour se reposer seurement*" ["In order that faith may find in Jesus Christ a firm basis of salvation on which it can take its stand with certainty"] (2). And it was certainly because of its helpfulness in preaching and teaching that in later days not only the Reformed confessions and systems of dogmatics but also the Lutheran, Anglican and even Roman Catholic theologians have adopted it.

The doctrine of the threefold office teaches that Christ is Prophet, Priest and King. But it does not mean by this that Christ is first Prophet, then Priest and finally King, though there is a certain correspondence between these titles and the ministry of Christ, his crucifixion and his glorification. The three offices are so related to one another that Christ is Prophet in a priestly and royal manner; Priest in a prophetic and royal way; King, but King as priest and prophet.

The three offices can be distinguished; they cannot be separated. At every moment Christ acts in all three capacities: The Prophet teaches with authority and announces his death; the Priest sacrifices himself, proclaims God's forgiveness and conquers death; the King reigns through his word and (in the old Christian phrase) from the Cross (3). As Prophet he enlightens our ignorance, as Priest he overcomes our alienation from God, as King he turns our impotence into victory (4). But it is all one work of salvation. It is, therefore, not permissible to emphasize one of the three offices to such an extent that the other two are forgotten. A one-sided emphasis on the prophetic ministry leads inevitably to moralism and rationalism: Christ becomes a great teacher of ideas and principles, but his work, past, present and future, disappears from the horizon. An exclusive emphasis on the priestly function leads to pietism and mysticism: Christ is the Lamb of God, but his piercing word and his victory over sin and death are not taken seriously. The full concentration on the Kingship of Christ leads to utopianism and apocalypticism. Christ is the glorious King, but it is forgotten that his victory is the invisible victory of the word and that in this world the road to glory is the way of the Cross.

It is, however, one thing to maintain that the three

offices are inseparable and need equal emphasis; it is another to apply this principle consistently all along the line. Again and again in the history of theology we find that one or the other of the three aspects of Christ's work claims almost exclusive attention. This is not necessarily wrong. A generation of theologians may be called upon to throw full light on that part of the work of Christ which has not been sufficiently illuminated by previous generations. But such one-sidedness leads to a derailment of theology with all its dangerous consequences for the faith and life of the Church, if it implies neglect or even negation of the other aspects of Christ's work for men. For in that case the whole structure of theology and consequently of the preaching of the Church loses its sense of pro-portion and of perspective. The Church cannot live with a truncated gospel. Thank God the Church is never left without the help of His Word and sooner or later that Word imposes itself again in its fullness. The history of theology and of preaching is a long series of battles of the full Gospel against the partial and one-sided gospels.

We are today in the midst of one of these battles.

Protestantism stands in a theological tradition in which the priestly and prophetic ministries of Christ have been strongly worked out but in which the kingly office has been obscured. The cosmic Christ, who is not only the Lord of the Church but the present though invisible ruler of the universe, to whom all power is given in heaven and on earth (5), who has triumphed over all powers (6), under whose feet all things have been put (7) and who will return in glory, has not been proclaimed among us as he has been proclaimed by the apostles. The words spoken in another connection by Comenius when he passed on the "Bequest of the Unity of Brethren" are still to find their fulfillment: "Christ must find among you not only a pulpit for His prophetic office; not only an altar for His office as priest and bishop; but likewise a throne and a sceptre for His kingly office " (8). We are, therefore, called to render witness in a special way to Christ the King and to interpret the full cosmic significance of the history of salvation. This does not mean that we can afford to forget the prophetic and priestly Christ, but it does mean that we seek to rediscover the royal nature of our prophetic and priestly Lord.

If we survey the history of Protestant theology in this respect we find, first of all, that the Reformers are more reserved in their teaching concerning the Kingship of Christ than they are about his other

offices. Both Luther and Calvin show a certain hesitation with regard to the cosmic aspects of Biblical
eschatology. Their struggle against the different apoc-
alyptic sects with their anarchistic political implications made them overcautious in their attitude to the
world-wide historical and suprahistorical perspectives
of the Bible. It is typical that these two tireless inter-
preters of the Bible have not given us commentaries
on the Book of Revelation (9).

Karl Barth has spoken of the overemphasis on the
pretemporal rather than postemporal in Reformation
theology. By this he means that the Reformers are
especially concerned with the basis and origin of salvation, which had to be restated over against their
distortions in medieval theology, rather than with its
fruit and goal (10). The result is that the world is not
sufficiently seen in the light of the victory of Christ.
The orders of creation come to occupy a larger place
than they have in the New Testament.

Luther's specific interest in this connection was to
overcome the confusion between the realm of Christ
and the realm of the world which had been created
by Roman clericalism and appeared in a different form
in the enthusiastic sects of the Reformation period (11). But in his desire to disentangle the cause
of Christ from the entangling alliances with papal

theocracy or anabaptist utopianism he came to distinguish the two realms so sharply that their fundamental togetherness under the Lordship of Christ is no longer clearly seen. Luther has given us some of the most powerful statements that have ever been made about the victory of Christ over all other powers. The author of "A Mighty Fortress" teaches not only that Christ governs the faithful in his Church but also that Christ governs the whole universe. Bishop Berggrav is surely right that it is a crude distortion of Luther to affirm that Christians owe allegiance to two different Lords (12). It is certainly not his teaching (what some of his later followers have tried to make him say and what many of his modern critics have attacked him for) that the political and social order are not subject to the divine commandments. Luther believes, as Hanns Lilje puts it, that "the earthly ruler must remember that in order to resist the temptation to rule arbitrarily, he is responsible for his royal office to the Lord of Lords and the King of Kings" (13). And Luther has acted on this conviction by recalling the rulers of his time in the strongest terms to their divine vocation. It remains, nevertheless, a fact that most often in Luther's own teaching and in a more pronounced form in later Lutheran theology the accent falls so heavily on the side of the *present* separation

of the two realms that the Church appears to be the
only realm in which, in this present dispensation,
Christ's Kingship is truly operative and relevant and
that no explicit theological foundation is laid for a
consistent witness by the Church concerning Christ's
Lordship in and over the world.

Calvin has given us more explicit teaching about
the royal office. Christ is "the Lieutenant of God,"
who governs heaven and earth on behalf of the Father.
"*Christ n'a pas été reçue aux cieux pour jouir d'un
repos bienheureux loin de nous, mais afin de présider
sur le monde pour le salut de tous fidèles*" ["Christ
has not been received in heaven in order to enjoy bliss-
ful rest far away from us, but in order to preside over
the world for the salvation of all the faithful"] (14).
All sovereignty on earth is, therefore, an image of the
Kingship of Jesus Christ. The throne of Christ is set
up among us in order that his heavenly voice may be
the only rule of life for rulers and subjects. The rulers
must, therefore, submit themselves to the great King
Jesus Christ (15). But while Calvin proclaims Christ's
Lordship so clearly, he does not always draw the consequences which should be drawn in this connection.
Thus in the fundamental passage of the *Institutio* (16)
where the doctrine of the Kingship of Christ is explained, he develops fully Christ's Lordship over the

Church, but does not use this opportunity to define in what sense and in what manner Christ is King of the world. Again in the other crucial passage where the place of the state in the plan of God is discussed there is no clear exposition of Christ's Lordship in the realm of society. On the contrary, we read: "*Le royaume spirituel de Christ et d'ordonnance civiles sont choses fort loin distantes l'une de l'autre*" ["The spiritual Kingdom of Christ and the civil order are things which are far away from each other"] (17).

How is this to be explained? There are in Calvin's teaching concerning the world two distinct trends. The world is sometimes seen from the angle of common grace and the law of nature. In that case the accent falls on the orders of creation; the world and the state exist as if in a realm by themselves (18). But this is not the dominating motive of his thought. The main accent falls on the universal sovereignty of Christ; the world and the state are conceived in a definitely Christocentric manner (19). It is possible to interpret Calvin as Dr. Kuyper has done in his Stone Lectures of 1898 as the advocate of a theocentric rather than a Christocentric view of the world and the political order and so to construct a "Calvinistic" theology of orders of creation in which the decisive word is not spoken by the Christ who

makes all things new. But it is certainly more true to
Calvin's own intentions to find in him, as Wilhelm
Niesel (20) has done, a Christocentric view of the
civil order based on the royal office of Christ, accord-
ing to which all government is rooted in the fact that
Jesus Christ sits at the right hand of God.

In the main Protestant confessions and theologies
of the succeeding period the threefold office of Christ
becomes a fixed doctrine. The three offices are generally mentioned, but here again it is remarkable that
the priestly office is most fully explained, the prophetic
office briefly mentioned and the royal office most
often defined in its relation to the Church but not
to the world. Blumhardt's complaint (21), that the
Reformation confessions are almost wholly silent concerning the return of the Lord and do not teach us
to expect him, is understandable. The full proportions
of the history of salvation are not adequately reflected
in the classical documents of Protestantism. They do
not call the Church to a persistent and joyful witness
concerning Christ's present Lordship in all realms of
life. The general tendency of Protestantism becomes,
therefore, more and more to describe the Reign of
Christ as an invisible, spiritual and heavenly reality
which is located in the *souls* of men (22). This shift

of emphasis from the universal, all-embracing sovereignty of Christ over the whole world to a purely inward sovereignty leads inevitably to the pietistic conception that the affairs of this world are the sole concern of the secular powers and that the Church has no word for the world but only for individuals who are to be saved out of this world. A voice such as that of Johann Georg Hamann—who wrote in the days of Voltaire and Frederick the Great that Christianity is above all a political sect because it has a King, who proclaims a Kingdom—remains a voice crying in the wilderness. The whole trend is in the other direction. Christianity becomes more and more introspective and the Church knows less and less what to do with the world-embracing and world-shaking affirmations of the Bible.

Schleiermacher gives clear expression to the non-cosmic, subjective conception of Christ's Kingship. His interpretation of the royal office confines it wholly and exclusively to the realm of the church. He rejects the doctrine that Christ governs the world (23): "Christ commands only the forces of the Church." The world is the realm in which God rules. In view of this definite separation the two realms have no right to intervene in each other's affairs. The Church should in no way concern itself with the civil order.

Christ is the end of all "political religion" as he is the end of all outward theocracy (24). Thus the Pantocrator has become the governor of a clearly limited province. Christ is no longer the main actor in the dramatic history of world salvation; he is the inspiration of a community of souls. It is, therefore, not to be wondered at that in the following period the Church finds it increasingly difficult to proclaim any relevant word to the world.

In the most influential schools of theology of the nineteenth century the dominating conception of Christ becomes that of Christ as Prophet. On the basis of the presupposition that "the people do not accept the supernatural" (25) and that all reality—divine or human—must be reduced to the level of one single reasonable and wholly explicable historical process, the generation of the great innovators could find no place for the seemingly superstitious conception of Christ as Priest and the seemingly fantastic faith in a cosmic Reign of Christ. They concentrated therefore all the more eagerly on the prophetic teacher. But now we see with astonishing clarity what it means to isolate one of the offices from the others. This prophet is no longer the priestly prophet whose word is confirmed by his sacrifice, nor the royal prophet who

overcomes the world even in and through his death.
This prophet announces timeless truth, principles and
ideas which are added to the treasure house of human
aspirations and insights, which lift man to greater
heights—but which make no fundamental difference
in man's condition. The "perfect idealism" of Jesus
with his "idyllic and sweet nature" (26) may give a
new glamour to human life. But it leaves man where
he is, imprisoned within a world in which his ideals
are impotent. Cromwell's word: "Jesus speaks things"
no longer holds, for after the birth, life and death of
this prophet nothing else remains than a new teaching
about God. "The course of the world has not been
changed by Jesus. . . . While Jesus has not brought
the Kingdom of God he has brought a new religion" (27). These sentences of Wernle express the
message of liberal theology in all its bareness. The
prophet who is not priest and king is only a teacher
of religious truth.

History according to these moderns is wholly and
exclusively governed by laws the nature of which is
generally known. All history is of one piece. The belief
of the evangelists and apostles that Jesus arose on
the third day and that he will return is therefore necessarily a naïve misunderstanding. "Let us forgive him
his hope in a glorious coming on the clouds of heaven,"

says Renan patronizingly. And again: "Let us not despise this chimera, which has been the crude husk of the sacred bulb by which we live" (28). This idea that the eschatological setting of the Gospel, its character as a witness about events which radically change the whole life of the world, in short, its significance as history of God's action, is no more than a shell which can be disregarded—this idea is echoed again and again in the following years. Nearly forty years after Renan, Harnack in his famous lectures on the "Essence of Christianity" makes the same point. According to him Jesus shared naturally the eschatological conceptions of his contemporaries, but "his own true property is that of the Kingdom which does not come with outward means" (29). Consequently the genuine abiding message of Jesus deals only with "God and the soul, the soul and its God." All the dramatic apparatus concerning world history and eschatology is a mere framework; what counts and remains is the purely spiritual and ideal message concerning God and the inner life of the individual. When a few years later the new school of history of religions comes up, Bousset (30) dismisses the expectation of the approaching end of the world in the same easy way by declaring that it is a "temporal cover of eternal thoughts."

The cosmic significance of Christ is denied, but a

desperate effort is nevertheless made to maintain that in view of the lofty spirituality of his teaching Jesus remains the incomparable and in that sense central personality of history. This standpoint becomes, however, untenable when the historical method is applied with complete consistency. This is shown by Ernst Troeltsch, the dominating figure of the period just before the First World War. For him the Kingdom of God is not "the utopian miracle of the future," but the "fellowship of humanity and of love of God" (31). Nothing in history is isolated or absolute. While we can continue to follow Jesus as the embodiment of "great religious energy," we must resolutely cease "to construe Jesus as the centre of the world or the centre of human history. . . . There can be no question of a cosmic place and significance of Jesus, as the Church's doctrine of incarnation and salvation has it" (32). In his *Glaubenslehre* Troeltsch goes even farther and states: "A modern theologian says that in our days the eschatological bureau is generally closed. It is closed because the ideas on which it was based have lost their roots" (33). Troeltsch himself confesses that of the three offices the modern conception finds that of the prophet "the most serviceable" (*verwertbar*) (34).

We see now the full meaning of that reduction.

The doctrine of the threefold office was meant to describe the world-embracing, world-transforming work of Christ. There now remains only a message, and a message which, however sublime, leaves the ultimate problems of human destiny and of God's purpose with the world unanswered. The Church is left alone with itself—without a King.

It is true that in these same days there arose a reaction among Biblical scholars against the liberal, un-eschatological image of Jesus. Johannes Weisz and Albert Schweitzer denied that eschatology was merely an accidental element in the thought and teaching of Jesus and maintained that the message of the impending arrival of the Kingdom was the very heart of the Gospel. They took it, however, for granted that no reasonable modern man could possibly accept this eschatological conception of life and so their discovery resulted rather in undermining liberal theology than in pointing the way to a new Biblical theology. Those of us who were in the theological faculties in the years immediately following the First World War have grown up in that atmosphere of extreme uncertainty. All roads seemed to be blocked. Orthodoxy and modernism were equally discredited. Christ the Priest and Christ the King seemed to have abdicated. And Christ the Prophet had left us a message which was incomprehensible to modern man and had therefore to be radically modified in order to become applicable to our condition. We wondered whether the Church could live, whether the preachers could witness, if their message was no more than a reference to ideals which did not seem to have any foundation in history and in the realities of the universe.

It was in those days that new voices began to be heard, voices of men who had themselves agonized over the theological impasse, men who realized the crying need of the chaotic postwar world for a clear word of guidance and the tragic impotence of the Church.

The most impressive and widely influential voice was that of Karl Barth. Not the only one. As Asmussen says (35), Barth became the speaker for men of many different backgrounds who were struggling to find a true and certain word. Thus in those same years we find in many countries a new concern with the Reformers. In France we hear of a turning "from Fosdick to Pascal." The two Blumhardts, who in their time had been somewhat esoteric prophets of a nonpietistic and truly cosmic, nonindividualistic and fully eschatological witness, now began to be heard and understood. In their own time they had been almost alone in proclaiming the actual Kingship of Christ. "If the main point (*Hauptpunkt*) becomes uncertain: the notion of the Kingdom, the results of theological science do not amount to much," Blumhardt, Jr., had written. "The King is Christ, not the state, which has power over you, not Protestantism or Catholicism, not even the doctrine about Christ which you may construe." "He has been crowned three times; he has died, he is risen and he sits at the right hand of God. He does not give up his death, his life, his throne. That is the great promise, which we have in him; in this light our past, our present and our future is dominated by hope (*in Hoffnung gestellt*)" (36). In the great uncertainty of the postwar era this message suddenly struck home.

The dialectical school became the spearhead of the new battle against the dissolution of theology into history and psychology. It was inevitable that the protest should take the form of a thorough attack on the immanentism of the previous generation. The way had to be cleared for the freedom of God's Word, for its objectivity, for its transcendence. Barth set out to disentangle the Gospel from the entangling alliances and presented it in its otherness, its strangeness. The Bible became again the Word that had not arisen in the hearts of man, the Word which is not to be handled according to our arbitrary presuppositions, but which speaks with ultimate authority.

The new theologians accepted the conclusion of the historians and critics that the New Testament message is essentially eschatological in character. But they did not regard this discovery as a sterile scientific truth or as an obstacle to be overcome. The stone that their predecessors had rejected became for them the cornerstone of the building. The stark contrast between the present age and the age to come, between the old and the new creature, which had seemed so completely antiquated was now seen to be the saving word, which spoke to the condition of modern man.

But what did the dialectical school understand by eschatology? In the early stage Barth and his associates did not conceive of it in terms of the last things but in terms of the eternal things. It is the vertical situation that matters. If eschatology is the very heart of the Gospel, man is permanently in the situation of crisis, in which the eternal holy God judges his finite sinful existence and in which salvation consists in accepting that critical situation in all its consequences. The eschatological orientation is not directed toward events in the temporal or posttemporal order. The return of Christ is not a historical event. The Gospel confronts man "here and now" and always with the suprahistorical Word of judgment and salvation. Every moment is a moment of decision in which the "no" and "yes" of God is addressed to us.

All times or ages are, therefore, contemporaneous with the Kingdom of God (37). And we must see every period of history as a time when the end is near (38). In so far there is no *history* of salvation but an eternal *moment* of salvation. The coming age and the Kingdom of God do not represent a future event but an eternal presence.

Thus the closed universe of the immanentists is broken through. Man stands once again before the living God. The Church is not to concern itself with the relativities of history and psychology, but to announce the other world, the world beyond history. In his address on "The Church and Culture" (1926) Barth says: "We suffer from a nearly total neglect of the consolation and the warning of eternity, from an altogether fatal lack of knowledge concerning God as our limit and concerning the returning Christ, Who says 'I make all things new.'" He adds that the Church has today the specific task to proclaim what the "*regnum gloriae*," the Reign of the victorious King, means and that the Ecumenical Conference of Stockholm would have found another message, if the churches had not lost this vision. The churches can only be healed by learning to *hope*.

Barth has indeed taught many what *hope* means. The doors of the prison of historical and psychological determinism were opened. And through them we could see again a glimpse of the other, the eternal world in its dangerous holiness and its awful glory.

Witness was rendered once again to Christ the King. Emil Brunner wrote: "To believe means to receive a Lord, a King, who is really, unconditionally King, absolute King, excluding all democracy. The whole revelation is nothing else than the divine reconquering of the rebellious province. Regem habemus. The time of anarchy is past" (39). The sense of certainty and gratitude which is expressed by this word of Brunner was the great gift which the new theology gave to many of the younger generation in the twenties. From afar the theology of crisis appeared to be a message of despair and of quietism. But for those who accepted it, it became a message of joy and a call to go forward. The overwhelming dimensions of God's world-embracing plan began to dawn on them.

But in that first period their radical dualism between time and eternity did not allow the dialectical theologians to show how this hope transformed the life of men in this world. No one has indicated this more clearly than Barth himself in his criticisms made in more recent years of his early writings (40). The unilateral emphasis on eternity as the limit of time, on the vertical as over against the horizontal, made it impossible to show what bearing God's history has upon human history. All history seemed equally relative, all decisions equally finite and therefore sinful. And what was even more dangerous, the Biblical view of the history of God as an eventful history in which God carries out His design, in which, therefore, each age or dispensation has its specific place and function, was replaced by a static conception of history in which there is no differentiation, in which, precisely because the same crisis takes place at all times, the specific crises of the incarnation, of the crucifixion, of the resurrection, of the coming of Jesus Christ in glory lose their truly critical character.

And this could only mean that the problem of ethics could not find a clear answer. The Kingship of Christ according to the younger Barth was in danger of being understood as the rule of a King who judges and pardons indiscriminately and to whom all action in the realm of human affairs is equally irrelevant.

The new theology had resulted in a great spring cleaning and in a purifying of the atmosphere but it was as yet too abstract, too much "in the air" to help the Church find a fully Biblical and relevant message for the world. Its function so far had been largely negative, namely, to break the spell of monolithic immanentism. The question was whether it would remain a necessary reaction against the modernist reaction or whether it would result in the rediscovery of the Biblical witness in all its fullness and concreteness.

~~~~~~~~~~~~~ CHAPTER II ~~~~~~~~~~~~~

The Proclamation of the Kingship of
Christ in the Years of Struggle

~~~~~~

The period between the two world wars was one of
intense theological activity. The deadlock between
scientific Biblical studies and systematic theology was
being broken. It was increasingly understood that the
Bible had to be read in the light of its own presuppositions. And so the Biblical Words were once again
understood as bearers of *the* Word. The fundamental
unity of the Old and New Testament was rediscovered. As the rationalistic prejudices which had been
the main obstacles to a real understanding of the Bible
were attacked one by one, the way was paved for a

38

return to a Biblical—but not Biblicist or fundamentalist—theology. Theology ceased to be an appendix to other disciplines and began again to follow its own specific laws.

But this by no means implied that the witness and life of the Church were transformed. In fact the battle for that transformation had not yet really begun. So far the new theology had been mainly a matter of passionate debate among the theologians, not yet a revolutionary force in the Church. It is true that an increasing number of pastors had learned again that preaching is not the lecturing about religious ideas and experiences, but the transmitting of the living Word of God. But much of this preaching consisted in undigested doctrinal statements, was lacking in concreteness and did not, therefore, affect the faith and life of church members. The churches as a whole had not yet heard and even less understood the real challenge which was implicit in the new theology.

This was a fortiori true concerning the relation of the churches to the world. At the Stockholm Conference of 1925 most European theologians were quite outspoken in their criticism of the "social gospel theology" of many of their American fellow delegates, but had little to offer in its place. In the critical years around 1930 the European churches remained largely

silent concerning the vital issues of society and of the
international order. What Professor Heering wrote in
1932 was uncomfortably true: "The ruling Orthodoxy
as well as the current modernism of our time have lost
the Christian prophetic sense" (41).

The relative impotence of the new theologians to
make their theology relevant to this situation was
largely due to the fact that they had first of all to
concentrate upon the clarifying of their fundamental
theological position. They were not yet ready for the
affirmation of its full implications for church and
world. But—as was to come out later—this battle
about the fundamentals was by no means as academic
as it appeared to be. It was in those last years before
the crucial date 1933 that the main theological decisions were made which would show their fruits in the
years of conflict.

Some (including several former associates of Barth)
turned with new enthusiasm to a theology of the
orders of creation, in which nation and state received
a sanctity that could only serve the greater glory of
the rising nationalism. In the theology of Karl Barth
and his associates there occurs, however, in these same
years a very different development. This development
is characterized first of all by the fact that the "Christian dogmatics" of 1927 are transformed into the

"Church dogmatics" of 1932, for dogmatics are now understood as a task to be accomplished in and for the Church. Dialectical theology is no longer merely critical theology. It seeks to formulate the truth which the church as a whole should proclaim. In the second place the development is toward a radical Christocentricity. All natural theology—all attempts to base theology on anything else except the fact of Christ—is rejected as parasitical. But this does not mean an even more outspoken otherworldliness or an even more decided relativizing of the realities of this world. On the contrary. The otherworldly and radically dualistic eschatology, which could so easily be understood as a complete negation of the present world (42), is modified. Christ has overcome the world and is already King of kings and Lord of lords. The road from "nature" to a social gospel is forbidden. But we do not need to take that road. For the gospel of grace, of the Lordship of Christ, contains good news for the world and leads itself to a cosmic witness (43). The concentration upon the unique revelation proves to be the point of departure from which a wide expansion is possible.

But it was not only the Barthians who rediscovered the dimensions of Biblical theology. In 1931 Aulen, the leader of the renewal in Swedish theology, pub-

lished his study on the atonement which was translated under the title *Christus Victor*. Its main thesis
is that, according to the "classic" conception, atonement is a divine conflict and victory. The victorious
Christ fights against and triumphs over the evil powers
of the world and thus God reconciles the world unto
Himself. This means that the drama of salvation is
seen in its wider cosmic content and that atonement
is no longer described in individualistic categories.

At the same time the theologians of the Russian
emigration began to make their influence felt. Through
them European theology was brought in contact with
that great stream of Christian thought which had
retained the eschatological outlook of the early Church
and which had not gone through the process of reduction and secularization of Western European history.
Their comprehensive theological systems were received
with critical reserve, but they helped considerably in
widening the horizons of European theology and in
bringing it back to the universal Gospel of the primitive Church. The Orthodox Church prays in its Easter
liturgy: "All creation doth celebrate the Resurrection
of Christ, on whom also it is founded." It was this
sense of the all-embracing significance of Christ's victory which Orthodoxy contributed to the West.

In these ways the ground was being prepared for

the period in which everything would depend on the presence of a Church which would know nothing but Christ and him crucified—and would counter the totalitarian claims with the total claim of Christ. As one looks back on the whole development of the pre-Nazi period in Europe one sees, besides much uncertainty and vain theological debating, also clear indications of the way in which the Lord of the Church was preparing for his people the weapons which they would need in the decisive hour.

The significance of the German Church struggle for the theological development cannot easily be exaggerated. For in that struggle the new theology came to grips with the realities of the life of the Church and of the world. The great challenge thrown down by aggressive paganism forced theology to descend into the arena and to work out a clear and relevant message concerning the nature of the Church and its function in the world.

The attack upon the Church did not take the form of a straightforward attempt to abolish it. The danger consisted precisely in its indirect and insidious character. National Socialism used three different methods: firstly it attempted to persuade the Church to mix a strong dose of National Socialist ideology with its

Christian tradition; secondly it sought to force the Church to reshape its order according to the Nazi pattern; thirdly it tried to cut the Church off from the general life of the nation. The situation was particularly serious because a considerable section of church leaders and church members proved an easy prey for the new movement with its powerful propaganda. And this was not astonishing. If the Nazis proposed the abolition of the Old Testament, could they not call up great modern theologians as witnesses of the crown? If they desired to introduce the Führer principle in the Church could they not take their stand on the caesaropapism which had been accepted for so long by the German churches? And if they declared that the Church had nothing to do with the social and political order, were they not repeating in a somewhat crude fashion what many theologians had declared to be one of the greatest discoveries of the Reformation? The Nazis were drawing the ultimate consequence of the dethronement of Christ the King. Since the world, theology and the Church itself had become lordless, why not set up a new sovereignty?

Over against this attack upon its very substance the real Church, if there was still a real Church, could only answer by a radical affirmation of the unique and exclusive Lordship of Christ. The significance of the

Barmen declaration of 1934, the decisive utterance of the Confessing Church, was precisely that it affirmed this Lordship in unmistakably clear and incisive language. Confronting, as it did, the danger that Christ should be preached together with other lords, that the Gospel should be proclaimed in syncretistic mixture with pagan "isms," Barmen said simply: The Church preaches the Lord Christ alone. This is the crucial statement: "Jesus Christ, as He is proclaimed in Holy Scripture, is the one Word of God, to which we have to listen, and which we have to trust and to obey in life and death." From this radically Christocentric confession it follows that the Church rejects all other powers or ideas which pretend to supplement the one unique source of its witness. It follows also that it is unthinkable that Christians should be subject to Jesus Christ in one realm and to other lords in other realms. The Church belongs to Christ and to him alone and cannot possibly leave its order to be shaped according to the changing ideologies of the world. The state has a specific divine vocation but the doctrine that it is the sole and total order of human life is a pernicious heresy.

We have here a remarkably clear affirmation of the exclusive Lordship of Christ. All "both . . . and" theology, all attempts to improve on God's revelation in

Christ by an admixture of natural theology or reason, or modern ideals, or racial intuitions, are cut off at the root. And we have this witness in such an incisive form that it becomes highly relevant to the life of the Church and indeed of the world. The Lordship of Christ is proclaimed as a dynamic truth which is to govern the Church and its members in decisions of life and death.

Barmen became the starting point for the struggle of the Church to defend its faith and order against the invasion of the National Socialist ideology. In that struggle the Confessing Church did not always live up to the faith which it had confessed. There were periods of great uncertainty, there were compromises, there were acts of treason. But the Confessing Church lived on in spite of its weaknesses because the truth that the Church belongs to Jesus Christ alone found again and again its defenders, its witnesses and even its martyrs. There is in the public utterances of the synods of the Confessing Church of the critical years a note of joyful assurance that the Lord of the Church gathers his people all the more certainly when the Church is under fire. The Synod at Augsburg in 1935 says simply: "We praise under the Cross the victory of the Lord." And Pastor Iwand writes in 1936 (44) about the early years of the struggle: "God's Word reassembled the people, it strengthened the confessing Christians, it gave to leaders and pastors the armour of the spirit; the Scripture was opened up as had not happened for a long time, for the Lord Himself was among us with His word and His spirit." And even though in the weariness and strain of the long years of battle there came times when the Church was not only hard pressed on the outside but uncertain in its own message, it was finally the gospel of the victory of Christ which saved it from being crushed by the forces of paganism.

To carry out the Barmen declaration in its full implications would have meant, however, to start a battle all along the line in which the Church would not only defend its own purity but also counteract the totalitarian claim of National Socialism with the even more comprehensive and absolute gospel of the Kingship of Christ. It cannot be said that this has really happened. The Confessing Church has on the whole fought a defensive rather than an aggressive battle and concentrated its attention so largely on the issues of Church life that the wider issue of the battle for the nation and for the world has been neglected. Why did this happen? Why did the strong word spoken at Barmen not lead to the emergence of a truly prophetic Church?

There are several reasons. In the first place the demonic character of National Socialism was at first not fully understood by Christians in Germany, as it was not understood by Christians outside Germany. Moreover the Church found itself in so weak a position that it had to begin with the beginning, namely, to restore its own identity as a Church. Theology had not yet come to grips with the issues of the world. Karl Barth had written in 1933 that his fight against the German Christians had nothing to do with his political attitude to National Socialism (45) and that the recognition of the powers ordained by God is "selfevident" (46). His motive in making these statements, which he was to qualify so thoroughly in later years, was to make clear that the counterattack against the German Christians was in the first instance a theological concern. But many others in the Confessing Church systematized the distinction between theology and politics to the extent of a complete separation between the two spheres. Using once again the doctrine of the two realms, but forgetting that that doctrine referred originally to the different functions of the Christian Church and the *Christian* prince, they maintained that the resistance against National Socialism in the spiritual realm could go together with unreserved loyalty in the political realm. How far even

"orthodox" theologians could go in this matter is illus-
trated in that astonishing document, the *Ansbacher
Ratschlag*, in which well-known church leaders thank
God "that he has given us in our need the Führer as
a pious and faithful overlord and that he prepares for
us in national socialism good government with dis-
cipline and honour" (47).

The Confessing Church as a whole has never overcome the limitations implicit in its beginnings and
has, therefore, not consistently preached the Kingship
of Christ in its all-embracing consequences. But the
truth proclaimed at Barmen that Christ is the only
Lord to be served could not be imprisoned within the
walls of the Church. Again and again it has broken
out in the declarations of church councils. We can
give only a few examples. Thus the Confession Synod
of the Old Prussian Union in Dahlem said in 1935:
"Bound to God's Word the Church is obliged to witness before state and nation to the unique sovereignty
of Jesus Christ, who alone has the power to bind and
loose consciences" (48). In 1936 the Provisional Government of the Confessing Church sent an extremely
strong letter of protest to the Führer with specific
reference to the misdeeds of the National Socialist
party in all realms of life. The letter was followed by
a public declaration in which we read: "We pray all

rulers of our nation to remember seriously that they
will have to render account of all that they do to the
loving God. We adjure them to do nothing, to allow
nothing which goes against God's commandment
and against the freedom of consciences bound to
God" (49). The Confession Synod of the Old Prussian Union declared in 1938: "Where the Church is
hindered in its proclamation of Jesus Christ as Judge
and Saviour of the whole world, it must nevertheless
continue to deliver this message. . . . Before the judgment seat of God all will be revealed; the rulers and
the subjects" (50). And in the midst of the war, in
1943, the Confession Synod of Schleswig-Holstein
declared: "The Church cannot recognise the existence of realms which are a law to themselves and are
not subject to the Lordship of Christ. . . . The Church
would deny its confession, if it seeks refuge away from
public life and maintains silence concerning the claim
of the Lord Jesus Christ in judgment and grace over
the issues of political and national life such as war,
law, economics" (51).

The fighting Church owed a great deal to the theological renewal of the preceding years. But now the
need of the Church forced the theologians to face new
issues. What had theology to say about this grave

question of the attitude of the Church to an increasingly pagan, increasingly absolutist state? Some took refuge in the old doctrine of the orders and stretched it to the point where a completely free hand was given to the state, however pagan, in the earthly sphere. Many retired into the fortress of a purely interior, spiritualized, individualistic and eschatological pietism. But there were also those in the Confessing Church who understood that new answers had to be given. The struggle to find theologically true answers to the new questions is reflected in the work of Karl Barth. When Barth gives his exposition of the Apostolic Creed (1935) he shows that there are different "times," that there is a history of God which moves from one decisive date to another. There is a crisis of all history, but there are also crises within history. The volume of his *Dogmatics* which appeared in 1938 contains a specific warning against the impression created by certain passages of his *Epistle to the Romans* according to which revelation does not really enter into time but continues to transcend time. As Barth now reflects upon "the miracle of Christmas" and develops the implications of the incarnation, he is led to emphasize that, if the Word has become flesh, it has also "become time" (52). History is not a night in which all cats are gray. It is the realm into which

God's Word enters concretely and in which, therefore, concrete decisions for or against God have to be
taken.

In his Gifford Lectures of 1937 and 1938 Barth
draws the full consequences from this insight. He
remains the theologian of the unique revelation and
of that revelation alone, but he now retraces the rays
of light which that revelation throws on the life of
man in this world. Thus he speaks of a "political
service of God," which consists in the proclamation
of Christ's Lordship over all realms of life. "There is
fundamentally nobody and nothing in the world, to
which the Church does not owe its witness, namely
the witness of the threefold office of Jesus Christ"
(53). In the volume of the Dogmatics of 1940 it becomes clear why Barth has been forced to reformulate
his eschatology. Looking back he sees that the "theology of crisis" in its early stages could indeed be
understood as a theology of the eternal "no" to
humanity and of a transcendent hope which remained
wholly otherwordly. It had been too much a reaction
against the uneschatological thought of liberalism.
But the truths of God as the beginning, God as the
Lord of time, God as the end of time are equally to
be emphasized. Therefore, the life of man in time and
history, the question of ethics, the problem of Church

and state must occupy the attention of theology. And this not in order to return from a futuristic eschatology to some new immanentism but in order to do justice to the whole Gospel of God who is, who was and who will be (54).

Not many months after the occupation of Norway a new Church conflict broke out. But in this case the initiative came from the Church itself. For the Norwegian Church leaders did not wait until the Church was attacked. At a time when there were as yet no signs of interference with the life of the Church but when, in the life of the nation, law and justice were threatened, the Church spoke out. And so its witness did not deal in the first place with the rights of the Church but with the duties of the state. The first memorable document of the struggle was a sharp protest against the activities of the National Socialist youth organization and against the circumstances which had led to the resignation of the Supreme Court.

What was the theological basis of this action? The memorandum presented by the bishops almost immediately after their first protest begins thus: "In the second article of faith Christians confess Jesus Christ as their Lord, totally and without reserve. The duty to be obedient to Him stands for the Church above everything else." On the basis of this unequivocal declaration the bishops affirm that the Church cannot be silent where God's commandments are transgressed, for the Church is the guardian of the conscience. In view of this mission the bishops admonish the authorities to refrain from actions which contradict the order of God and to build the state on the unshakable divine law.

It is interesting to note that the Norwegian Church leaders in taking this stand call upon Luther as their main witness. Luther, says Bishop Berggrav, became in the years 1941-1942 one of our main weapons in the struggle (55). In a lecture which Bishop Berggrav gave in those days and which was circulated illegally, he explains this in the following manner: "Luther has not separated the two realms in such a way, that they must be two worlds without relation to each other. They have each their mandate, but they have the same mandator, who decides their aim. The government stands under the law of God. The church must not be the government, but it must proclaim the law of God to the government" (56).

In the succeeding stages of the Church conflict this position was fully maintained. Thus in 1942 the theological faculty of Oslo declared: "It is the duty and the right of the Church to see to it that the order and the laws of the state are in harmony with the will of God." The state "must listen to the criticism and warnings of the Church, if the Church accomplishes its task as guardian of the gospel and of the commandments of God." In the historic document of Easter, 1942, which was read from the pulpits and which bears the title, "The Basis of the Church," the Norwegian pastors quote the text from Ezekiel: "Son of man I have made thee a watchman unto the house of Israel; therefore hear the word at my mouth, and give them warning from me," and they affirm that, whenever the state is no longer a state according to God's Will, the Church must address the word of truth to it.

These are remarkable statements. For they go far beyond the traditional statements of the Lutheran doctrine concerning the two realms and are a clear refutation of its modern exposition in the theology of such influential teachers as Althaus and Elert. The Norwegian documents mention the doctrine of the two realms repeatedly. They insist that the Church is not to interfere in the state in temporal matters and that the state cannot be lord over the souls of men. But they do not deduce from this that Church and state are absolutely separate from each other and that the realm of politics is wholly autonomous. Over against the static dualism of those who teach that "Christianity has neither a political programme nor is it called to supervise or censure political life in the name of Jesus and the Gospel" (57), the Norwegian churchmen affirm simply and clearly: "The Church is the conscience of the state" (58). Professor Einar Molland has shown that this rediscovery of the prophetic office of the Church means a break with the main stream of the Lutheran tradition. He agrees, however, with Bishop Berggrav that it is in line with some of Luther's own sayings and that it finds powerful support in the wider tradition of the Christian Church. He closes his study of the theological implications of the Norwegian Church conflict by saying that in this matter the churches are moving forward to an ecumenical consensus. We can add that the teaching and especially the actions of the Norwegian Church have rendered an invaluable service in reminding the other churches of the simple but long-forgotten truth that the Church is to proclaim the Gospel and the Law in all realms of life.

The Norwegian conflict was followed by that in Holland. There also the Church took the initiative. Although the Netherlands Reformed Church had become sadly disorganized and without a message for the nation as a whole, it received at the decisive moment a relevant word and the courage to proclaim it to the people.

In the first period, in which the Church had to concentrate on the defense of the persecuted Jews, the official declarations were still lacking in clarity. The Church makes its appeal to the National Socialist authorities on the basis of Christian mercy, justice and love but it does not yet speak with that specific authority which comes from a proclamation of the total Lordship of Christ. But in 1943 there appeared illegally a brochure which gave clear expression to the convictions which should underlie the spiritual resistance of the Church. It contains these central affirmations: "The Lord of the Church is the Lord of the World; His Gospel is for all who live on this earth." "We reject as a deadly error the belief that the Kingdom of God is concerned only with the soul and eternity and that any other Kingdom may claim us for this earthy life" (59).

Not many months later the General Synod of the Netherlands Reformed Church issued a pastoral letter which strikes the same clear note: "It is the holy calling and the glorious privilege of the Church to bear witness to this high priest and king. . . . He has said: All power is given unto me in heaven and earth. This power is irresistible and the thought that this power can be expelled from any sphere of life is foolish unbelief. Therefore, the Church of Christ cannot cease making its voice heard in the whole realm of life . . ." (60). This was developed in relation to the state: "The authorities are subjects of the King of Kings, by whose grace they rule and to whom authorities and subjects alike owe obedience" (61).

Even more explicit are the theses of 1943 drawn up by Dr. Miskotte which became the basis for the attempt to bring the various parties and tendencies in the Church to a common confession of the faith. The fourth thesis says: "We recognize that the Church is called to proclaim Christ's kingship over the whole of life and to declare before the whole world that no sphere of life can withdraw with impunity from His powerful and loving majesty. The state as a legal system and society as a living organism can in fact not exist without Christ's Lordship. It is impossible to keep them from total disruption if they do not recognize His kingly rights based on His priestly sacrifice and revealed in His prophetic word" (62).

The significance of these statements is that they say explicitly what was implicit in the Barmen declaration. In its hour of need, when the utter defenselessness of

the Church became most manifest, the Church received again the one sufficient weapon—the simple
certainty that its Lord has overcome the world. At the
time when the world appeared to be wholly in the
hands of all-powerful destructive and diabolic forces,
the Church suddenly realized the full meaning of the
message of his victory and present Lordship.

This then is the precious gift which the Church—
in so far as it had ears to hear—has received in the
years of conflict. It can be formulated in two key
words: "The Lord of the Church is the Lord of the
world" and "The Church is the conscience of the
nation."

Neither during nor after the war have the churches
lived up to this rediscovery. But it has worked and will
work in them as a ferment which makes it difficult for
them to settle down again in the bad old ways of a
routine existence with a neat and comfortable delimi-
tation between the Church and the world. The history
of the last twenty years means for the Church that a
forgotten dimension of its faith has opened up. The
Church is not yet accustomed to the proportions of
the message which it is called to proclaim. Many
would like to go back to the smaller realm in which
the Church concerns itself only with individual souls,

with personal moral problems and with confessional documents of the past. They are frightened by the horizons which are opened up if the Kingship of Christ is taken seriously. They feel instinctively that this Kingship means complete reformation of the old sick churches and claims total revision of all Christian standards. But to try to forget the very King who has assembled, consoled and led his people in time of crisis is treason. The great question which faces the churches today is precisely whether they will, in gratitude for the gift bestowed on them, follow the King wherever he leads or prove ungrateful churches, whose light will have to be taken away.

In the short period which has elapsed since the war we have seen evidence that both these possibilities are real. Remarkable attempts have been made to give concrete expression to the faith that Christ is King of the Church and King of the world. But strong reactions against these attempts have come, not only from the side of secular public opinion, which was to be expected, but also from within the churches. Over against the demand for a consistent prophetic witness the slogan of the nonpolitical Church is heard once more. And the efforts to rebuild the life of the Church from the bottom upwards through the mobilization of the congregations are resisted by the partisans of mere restoration with their fear of renewal of any kind.

Thus the Stuttgart declaration of the Council of the German Evangelical Church, which was not only a word of repentance spoken for the sake of churches in other nations but also a call to Christians in Germany to make a radical new departure in obedience to Christ, a call for the reformation of the Church and for a clear witness to the nation, has not met with unanimous response in the churches in Germany. The long and passionate discussions which this declaration has caused show that it had touched the vital issue of postwar Germany, but they showed also that a large section of the Church has not understood what the Spirit had said to the Church through the time of suffering. There are many to whom the message of Stuttgart came as a great liberation, who take it as their basis for a new attitude in Church and state. But there are also many who react in a spirit of self-justification and so miss the great opportunity to start all over again in that newness of life which comes from having received forgiveness. It is clear that the future of the German Church depends on the outcome of this spiritual conflict. There is little hope for the German Church if the backward-looking forces win the day. But there is hope for it, and indeed for Germany, if the words spoken at Barmen and Stuttgart are filled with concrete substance, if they lead to a thorough reconsideration of the old theological positions and to a full confrontation with the Biblical message of the Kingship of Christ. We must therefore rejoice in hearing such statements as the one of the Synod of the Confessing Church of Berlin, which declares: "God Himself gives us the immeasurable task that all realms of life are to be ordered anew under the Word of God and the Lordship of Jesus Christ" (63).

But the situation is no different in other churches. We hear everywhere of efforts to break through the deadlock in the life of the Church. But we hear also of counterattacks in order to render these efforts ineffective. The Netherlands Reformed Church, which in its new provisional church order, adopted after the war, accepted its obligation "to render witness to the Gospel of Christ in relation to the government and the nation" and which has issued a number of messages and reports dealing with specific burning issues of public life, is faced by a strong reaction in its own midst of those who pretend that the Church is departing from its true spiritual function.

There is then no reason to speak in overconfident tones about the outcome of the meeting between the Church and its King. There is more reason for humble and repentant recognition of the fact that the Church represents a "stiff-necked people" which needs again and again to be called to order. But the fact of the meeting remains. And that itself is a reason for deep gratitude. The King has had his witnesses in our day and generation. The King has today his witnesses. So the question as to whether we want to join the company of those witnesses remains a question addressed to every one of us.

In closing this all too rapid survey of a theological development during the time of our own generation it is worth while to look at ourselves through the eyes of others.

In 1923 a Belgian Jesuit looking at the development of European Protestantism wrote that the Protestant return to the origins of the faith had proved to be a process of complete disintegration. The Protestant reduction had in fact become destruction and this was advancing at a rapid pace and would lead to the elimination of Christ as mediator (64).

In 1945 a French Jesuit surveying the religious scene wrote that Protestants and Catholics had both become disgusted with the denaturation of the salt of the earth. But he added that if Protestantism had gone farther in the direction of the secularization of

Christianity, it was today leading in the sense of a return to the eschatological perspectives (65).

These two statements help us to measure the distance which theology has traveled in the last quarter of a century. As always the Church has been slow to learn the lesson which God desired it to learn. In the midst of trial and judgment it has had to take the lesson to heart. The great question is now whether it will gratefully remember it and live by it or will once more forget it. The content of the lesson is that the Church belongs to a Lord who stands at the beginning, at the center and at the end of history.

CHAPTER III

The Kingship of Christ in the Bible

We must now try to develop what the Kingship of Christ means. And in the first of our three sections on this subject we begin by summarizing what we can learn from recent Biblical scholarship in this respect.

A specialist in higher criticism remarked recently that critical research, which in its early stages had removed Christ from the center of the Gospel, is now bringing us back to the simple truth that the whole New Testament message is a Gospel concerning Christ. In this way, he added, the Word of God has achieved a victory over the critics. Our task is to follow this development in one specific area and to show how Biblical criticism has been forced to rediscover the Kingship of Christ in the Bible.

The starting point is the recognition that the only adequate (and therefore the only scientific) way to deal with the Biblical record is to approach it as a record of witness. We have not to deal with a collection of historical essays or biographical studies, but with the proclamation of heralds, the teaching of evangelists, the exhortation of pastors. This is very obvious in the Acts of the Apostles and the Epistles but it is no less true of the Gospels, as their very name indicates and as a critical analysis of their structure and contents shows. The New Testament consists of preaching and preaching materials. The basic facts underlying this witness, the history which creates the proclamation, are not given to us in the form of the objective account of spectators, but communicated to us through the medium of a purposeful interpretation. Fact and interpretation are indeed so linked up with each other that we cannot possibly hope to make a clear separation between them. We must, therefore, make up our minds about the witness itself, including the facts and their interpretation by the apostles and evangelists.

The proper task of Biblical scholarship is, therefore,

not to discover first what is behind the witness and then to compare the naked facts with their interpretation. Since there is no objective extra-Biblical criterion which allows us to distinguish between the historical and the theological elments in the record, that method can only lead to arbitrary conclusions. The true task of criticism is rather to find the most original and primitive form of the Gospel of Christ and so to lead us as near to the fountainhead of the witness as possible. Considerable advance has been made in this field during recent years and the outline of the most primitive witness is becoming more and more clear.

What then is the rock bottom of the faith of the primitive Church? It is expressed in two words: *Jesous Kurios*, "Jesus is Lord." As we dig down deeper and deeper into the strata of the tradition we come finally to that simple affirmation.

This can be shown in two different and complementary ways. We can ask: What are the *common* elements in the oldest forms of witness which we have? Or we can ask: What are the *simplest* elements out of which the creed and liturgy of the Church have been built up? Following the first road we find that in the old Palestinian tradition as well as in the preaching of Paul the Lordship of Jesus is fundamental. This is clear not only in the use of the title "*Kurios*" in such central passages as Acts 2:21, and especially in Philippians 2, but also in the unique place which the 110th Psalm occupies in the whole primitive tradition. That Christ sits at the right hand of God, which means that he reigns as Lord, is the common faith of the Church of Jerusalem and of the Pauline churches. It was, therefore, a strange error to suppose that the title "Kurios" was introduced into the Church under Hellenistic auspices.

A study of the primitive credal or confessional formulas leads to the same conclusion. These formulas can be recognized by several characteristics. They are most often solemn statements which interfere with the normal flow of argument, and which summarize the main facts and truths of the faith. A very remarkable analysis of these statements has been made by Professor Cullmann (66). By reducing them to their common denominator and by working from the elaborate to the simple he comes finally to the two statements: "Jesus Christ is Lord" and "Jesus is Son of God." But, continuing his analysis, he finds that the first of these two is the more primitive and more fundamental. His conclusion is, therefore: "The affirmation that Christ reigns at present over the whole universe: that is the historical and dogmatic nucleus of the Christian creed. Its simplest expression is the formula: Kurios Christos" (67).

A study of the genealogy of the liturgical formulas leads to the same conclusion. The Aramaic "Maranatha" has certainly belonged to the oldest liturgy in Palestine (68). And the formulas for the Lord's Supper which Paul quotes in 1 Corinthians 11 as formulas which he has "received" point in the same direction.

But the question arises as to what the primitive tradition means by *Kurios*. Is the main analogy that of the lords of the Hellenistic world? Even if the expression is primitive, should we understand it in the light of the contemporary religions with their many lords, divine or human, their deities, rulers and saviors, forming together a weird and complicated pantheon? In that case the Lordship of Christ means no more than yet another apotheosis of a prophet or teacher. It is, however, very clear that nothing was farther from the thought of the New Testament authors. We have learned from the thorough lexicographical studies in Kittel's dictionary that the New Testament writers think in Old Testament categories and that, even when they use words which also belong to Hellenistic terminology, they use them in a Hebrew sense. The name given to Jesus is the name above every other name. The title "*Kurios*" is familiar to all readers of the Septuagint as the name of the Lord God Himself. And now that same most holy name is given to Jesus. The God besides whom there could be no other God,

the One and Only, has given to Jesus the place on
His right hand. The risen Christ is now the regent
of God's people, of God's world. He represents God
fully. Paul has no hesitation in quoting the word of
Joel: *"Everyone who invokes the name of the Lord
shall be saved"* (Romans 10:13) in order to under-
line the necessity of confessing, not the name of God,
but the name of the Lord Jesus. To him the destiny
of man, of the world, has been entrusted. Therefore,
the day of the Lord Yahweh, of which the prophets
spoke, now becomes the day of the Lord Jesus. And
the Jerusalem community prays to him: "Maranatha,
Lord come," while Stephen prays: "Lord Jesus, receive my spirit" (Acts 7:59).

The Lordship of Jesus Christ is then meant as an
absolutely unique Lordship. The primitive witness is
polemical. It takes its stand against the false lords and
affirms that Christ is Lord over all other lords. As
Ephesians 1:21 has it, "above all the angelic Rulers,
Authorities, Powers, and Lords, above every Name
that is to be named not only in this age but in the
age to come" (69).

More especially the polemic is addressed against
the worship of the emperor. Cullmann has shown that
the opposition in I Corinthians 12 between those who
say *"anathema Jesous"* and those who say *"Kurios*

Jesous" is very probably a reference to early persecutions in which Christians were forced to declare *"Kurios Kaisar"* and to deny their Lord Jesus. To accept the Lordship of Christ means then to accept the fact that he and he alone is the absolute master of the destiny of man and of the world; it means also to reject every other lord or master who pretends to have ultimate power.

It is precisely in the conflict with the many lordships of Hellenistic syncretism that the cosmic implications of the Lordship of Christ are worked out most clearly. The Epistles to the Ephesians and to the Colossians indicate the full proportions of what is involved in the resurrection and exaltation of Jesus. It is through him and unto him that all things have been created; it is through him that the world is reconciled unto God; it is toward the manifestation of his total victory that all history moves forward.

But what is the relation between this high doctrine and the seemingly much more simple witness which we find in the Synoptic Gospels? Even if it is granted that the oldest form of the kerugma which we can find culminates in the extraordinary claim of a cosmic Lordship, is it not possible that the more recently recorded Gospel story with its more immediate appeal contains a more original message?

In order to answer that question we must start from the central notion of the Kingdom of God. Israel had lived in the expectation that the Lord God would manifest His power by assuming Himself the immediate and direct reign over the world and by overcoming all inimical forces. Israel had looked forward to the coming of the Messiah who would bring the good tidings: "Thy God reigneth" (Isaiah 52:7). It is that same Reign of God which Jesus announces in the Gospel of the Kingdom. The uniqueness of his message is therefore not in the fact that he brings a new idea of the Kingdom, but in the fact that he proclaims that the Kingdom of God is near.

What does this nearness signify? Does it mean that the Reign of God, while approaching, is still wholly a matter of the future and that Jesus' coming, while representing a decisive stage in the proclamation of the Kingdom, is not itself a manifestation of the Kingdom? There are those who interpret the nearness of the Kingdom in such a manner. Now it is quite clear that the expressions concerning the approach of the Kingdom refer indeed to a coming event (70). It is equally clear, however, that this is not the whole truth about the Kingdom. In addition to the passages which represent the Kingdom as a promise, there are the many passages which speak of the Kingdom as a present reality. The Kingdom is now "in your midst" says Jesus (Luke 17:21). The text concerning the casting out of the daemons (Matthew 12:28; Luke 11:20) says: "If I cast out daemons by the Spirit of God, then the Reign of God has reached you already." The answer to the disciples of John the Baptist which quotes the prophetic description of the messianic age announces, to those who have ears to hear, that the promise of God is actually being fulfilled.

But how can the Kingdom be at the same time future and present, promise and fulfillment? The answer is implied in the last texts which we have mentioned as it is in the whole of the New Testament. The Kingdom is present in the Messiah. The Reign of God is revealed and actualized in the Evangel of His Son. Schniewind puts it very clearly thus: "Jesus is the messenger of good tidings who announces the Reign of God in such a way, that it becomes manifest in this proclamation" (71). But the same is true with regard to the actions of Christ. Their significance is that they reveal the actual victory of God over His adversaries. The Kingdom of God is still a matter of the future, because it is only existent in the words and deeds of Jesus. But it is a matter of the present because it is really among us in him. Kümmel's thorough analysis of the passages which are relevant in this connection can therefore lead up to the conclusion that "in Jesus the Reign of God has begun and in Him it will be accomplished. The promise of Jesus owes its certainty and its uniqueness to the fact, that it is fulfilled in Himself" (72).

This explains why we find both in the Gospels and in the Acts a number of passages which presuppose that Jesus and the Kingdom are identical. The saying of Mark (Mark 9:1) concerning the coming of God's Reign with power becomes in the Gospel of Matthew (Matthew 16:28) a saying about the coming of the Son of man (73). It is in this sense that Marcion says: "*In evangelio est Dei regnum Christus ipse*" ("In the gospel the kingdom of God is Christ himself") or that Origen coins the fine expression: "*autobasileia.*" Christ is not merely the herald of the Kingdom. In him the Kingdom is present among men. That is why there can be no competition between a Gospel of Christ and a Gospel about Christ. The two are inseparably bound up together.

Thus also it becomes clear what the Kingship of Christ means in the New Testament. The Reign of God is not only proclaimed. It is inaugurated. The anointed of God, the Messiah-King has come to reign on behalf of God. At first this tremendous event is still a secret. At first the Kingdom is proclaimed in

such a way that it remains an open question whether
Jesus is only its herald or whether he is also its King.
For Jesus is not the Messiah according to national
political dreams, but the hidden King, who is at the
same time the suffering servant. A direct self-revelation
would have brought a human, all too human, response,
and not the response of faith. He refuses therefore to
be made a King (John 6: 15). It is not by the votes of
men but by the act of God that he will ascend the
throne. But as the Cross draws near, the veil is gradu-
ally lifted. At the decisive moment he accepts the
royal title. And even then it must be made quite clear
that he is not a King according to man-made categories. "My Kingdom is not of this world"; that is to
say, it has its origin elsewhere; it is rooted in the design
of God. The Cross reveals that he is a priestly King
who dies for the people. His condemnation as King
of the Jews becomes precisely the full manifestation
of his true mission.

King of the Jews? Does that not mean that his
Kingship is far less universal than the Kurios title
seemed to suggest? No, for the King of Israel is, as
the Jews put it to Pilate, "the king messiah" (Luke
23: 2). He is the King who enters Jerusalem in the
Lord's name (Luke 19: 38). Though he occupies the
throne of David, he will reign not only over the house

of Jacob but over the whole world, for to his reign
there will be no end (Luke 1:32,33). He is the Son
of man to whom, according to the prophecy of Daniel
7:14, a kingdom is given which includes all peoples
and nations. The twenty-fifth chapter of St. Matthew
confirms this cosmic interpretation of Christ's Kingship. There the Son of man sitting on his throne of
glory and judging the nations is at the same time the
King. And the King is again the incarnate Lord who
speaks of the hungry, the thirsty, the strangers and
the prisoners as his brothers. As the sovereign judge
of the world identifies himself with the poor and the
needy, it becomes once more clear that his Kingship
differs utterly from the Kingship of the world. The
cosmic King is the prophet who knows no other
weapon than the Word of God and the priest who
gives his life as a ransom for many.

We can, therefore, say that there is no fundamental
difference between the two titles which we have briefly
analyzed. *Kurios* and *basileus* speak of the same reality
—of the fulfillment of the old promise that God Himself will establish His Reign. Both as Lord and as
King Christ is the fully adequate representative of
God.

In this matter there is no opposition between the
witness of the Acts and the Epistles on the one hand
and the Gospel on the other. The Acts and the Epistles

do not speak of Christ as King (74), but always as Lord. It is not easy to determine why this is so. It is probable that the name "Kurios" was felt to have even greater substance since it meant no less than that Christ is God. At the same time the title "Lord" was perhaps more easily understood by the pagan world, which could not understand the full implications of the history of the messianic Kingship. But whatever may have been the reason, it is quite clear that the reality of the Kingship is taken up in the witness concerning the victorious Lord. Thus Paul speaks of the "royal power" which Christ hands over to the Father in I Corinthians 15:24.

In the Book of Revelation the title "basileus" reappears again and in the closest relation with that of "Kurios." Christ is the Lord of lords and King of kings (Revelation 1:5; 17:14). Both names indicate that full authority and power have been given to Christ in heaven and on earth.

Is it possible to determine more clearly how we must understand this present Reign of Christ? Recent studies, in particular those of Cullmann (75), help us to overcome the vagueness of most theological thought on this point and to arrive at a more precise conception of this fundamental Biblical doctrine.

It is best to start again from the Old Testament

text, which is quoted so often in the New Testament that we are apt to consider it as a mere pious phrase, but which contains in fact a whole theology of history. We refer to Psalm 110: "The Lord said unto my Lord, Sit thou at my right hand, until I make thine enemies thy footstool" (Psalm 110:1). The verse is used again and again in the Synoptics, in the Acts, in the Pauline Epistles, in the Epistle to the Hebrews and in Revelation. It represents, therefore, a central common affirmation of all New Testament authors. What then does it mean? To sit at the right hand of God is to reign with God. This is stated explicitly in Revelation 3:21, where the Lord says that he has conquered and sat down beside the Father on His throne. Wherever this text is used we have a definite reference to the fact that Jesus has ascended the divine throne and that he is exercising his royal function, with regard not only to the Church, but also to the whole world.

We must, therefore, say that since the resurrection and the ascension we live in the dispensation of the Reign of Christ. This *basileia* of Christ is not to be confused with the *basileia* of God. God's Kingdom has been among us in Christ, but it remains nevertheless a promised, a future reality. Christ's Reign is here and now. This is explicitly stated in Colossians 1:13. God has rescued us "from the power of the Darkness" and transferred us "to the realm" (or Kingdom) "of his beloved Son." And in I Corinthians 15:24-28 Paul distinguishes clearly between the present dispensation in which Christ "must reign" and the ultimate hour of history when Christ will hand over his royal power to God the Father.

But Psalm 110 also speaks of victory over the enemies. It speaks of that victory as the *result* of Christ's Reign. Does this mean that Christ is not yet victorious at present? At this point we must be careful not to force the evidence, which seems at first very contradictory. For we find passages which speak of the victory as an eschatological promise and many others which describe the victory as a present reality. Is it possible to do justice to both or must we choose between a "futurist" and a "realized" eschatology?

There can be no doubt that the New Testament teaches that Christ *is* already victorious. "*Jesous Kurios*" does not mean that Jesus *will* be Lord some time in the future but that he *is* Lord and that he *has* overcome the world. This is already implied in the Gospels. Through his word and actions he actually overcomes the powers of evil. Satan is strong, but Jesus is the stronger one who invades Satan's realm, binds him (Matthew 12:29), overcomes him and takes his spoils away from him (Luke 11:20-22) (76). Satan's power is broken. Jesus sees him falling from heaven like a flash of lightning (Luke 10:18). The proclamation of the total victory of Jesus over the demonic powers, as a victory already achieved, becomes fully explicit on the basis of the gospel of the resurrection and the ascension. Thus the Epistle to the Ephesians declares that everything has been put under his feet, that is, all powers, good and bad (Ephesians 1:21,22). In Colossians we read the same, but it is added that he has exposed these forces and publicly triumphed over them (Colossians 2:10,15). And the first Epistle of Peter states that he went to heaven *after* the powers celestial had been made subject to him (I Peter 3:22).

The fact remains, however, that some passages seem to indicate that the victory is yet to be achieved. The second half of the text of Psalm 110 quoted several times implies that the victory comes at the end rather than the beginning of the reign (Acts 2:35). Now it is striking that the New Testament authors do not seem to feel that there is a contradiction between the victory achieved once for all and the victory still to be won. Thus the author of the Hebrews says in one passage that everything has been put under the feet of Christ (Hebrews 2:8) and in another that Christ at the right hand of God is waiting until his enemies are made a footstool for his feet (Hebrews 10:13).

What is the explanation of this ambiguity? The answer lies in the significance of the verb which is used again and again to indicate the nature of the victory: "*katargeo.*" The basic meaning of that verb (77) is "to render ineffective," to "demonetise," and its secondary meaning is "to crush" or "to annihilate." Now in most passages where the word appears in connection with the victory of Christ it is clearly used in the first meaning. A good example is I Corinthians 2:6. Moffatt translates it rightly and strikingly: "the dethroned Powers who rule this world." And that phrase contains the key to the solution of our problem. The inimical powers are no longer on the throne. There is only one throne and that throne is occupied. But they do not yet admit their defeat and are still acting as if they were the true rulers of the world. The victory is achieved in so far as the demonic forces are under control. But they still exist and the ultimate victory which will bring their total annihilation is therefore still to be won. Death is overcome in principle (II Timothy 1:10). It is still real, but it is no longer victorious and has lost its "sting" (I Corinthians 15:55). A symbolic way of describing this same situation is that Satan is "bound" (Mark 3:22-26). The adversaries of the Lord can only move within clearly defined limits. The decisive issue is settled. The victory already achieved is the guarantee for the ultimate and total victory. Paul can, therefore, write: "He must reign *until* all his foes are put under his feet. For God *has* put everything under his feet" (I Corinthians 15:23,27).

The time between the resurrection and the return of the Lord is then characterized by the fact that it is the time between the victory which is only known in faith and the manifest victory. We do not yet see all things put under his feet (Hebrews 2:8), but that does not change the fact that Jesus *is* the victorious Lord who rules over the whole universe.

As Théo Preyss has written: "There runs through the writings of the New Testament a sort of objective dialectic which results from the paradoxical situation of this intermediary time, this parenthesis in which the Church realises that it lives between the old world, defeated but still terribly aggressive, and the world to-come, already present in the resurrection of Jesus but still veiled and hidden to the eyes of man" (78).

The right understanding of the Biblical doctrine of Christ as Lord and King depends on the right insight into this togetherness of the two aeons or dispensations. The merely futurist interpretation leads to the undervaluing of the victory which is achieved and makes Christ a potential rather than a real King. But the interpretation according to which the total victory is already behind us leads to underestimating the reality of the adversaries, to the abandonment of hope and to the truncation of the history of salvation.

Let us look somewhat more closely at these two half-truths. For we have not to do with theological subtleties but with the insights upon which all further convictions and decisions concerning the Church and its function in the world ultimately depend. We can truthfully say to each other: "Tell me what your eschatology is and I will tell you what your attitude is in relation to Church, state and society." From the first beginnings of the modern ecumenical discussion at Stockholm until our own day this is the underlying theme to which we are forced back again and again. And let no one say that he has no place for eschatology, for there is no Christian faith which does not imply a conscious or unconscious conviction about the ultimate events and their relation to our present life and action.

The futurist interpretation of the Kingship seems at first glance very Biblical. Does not the Bible teach that the world is ruled by the Prince of this world? Does it not invite us to turn our eyes away from the world and toward the future event of the return of the

Lord? And must we not, therefore, conclude that in
the present dispensation we can only know Christ as
King of the Church? Those who answer these questions affirmatively can build up a very consistent
theology. They are no longer plagued by the problem
of the destiny of the world and of the function of the
Church in the world. For the world has no destiny.
The Church has no other function than to save men
out of the world. The result is that the two realms of
Church and world are separated by an unpassable
chasm and that the life of the Christian is split in two.

But this seemingly Biblical view does in fact violence
to the revelation. For it selects only one aspect of the
Biblical eschatology. The Bible speaks indeed of the
Prince of the world—but it emphasizes precisely that
the Prince of the world is *judged* (John 12:13; 16:11).
The Bible exhorts us indeed not to love the world, but
it proclaims at the same time that God so loves the
world that He has reconciled it to Himself. The Bible,
therefore, puts us in a historical situation in which we
must learn to distinguish between that which belongs
to "the present evil world" and that which announces
the world of the new creation breaking through in
Christ and in his Reign.

But the complementary half-truth is equally mis-
leading, if it is isolated from its context. It can also

base itself on Biblical data. Is not Christ risen? Does
that not mean that the victory has already taken place?
Must we not, therefore, cease to concern ourselves
with the future, which has nothing essential to offer
us, and concentrate rather on the exploitation of the
treasure which we have actually received? Must we not
consider that the Church is the Kingdom of God or
at least the beginnings of the Kingdom? And is it not
true that since the resurrection the world is transformed or at least beginning to be transformed? This
interpretation leads to an optimistic faith in the progressive penetration of the world by the forces of
Church and Kingdom. But it cuts the nerve of the
Biblical outlook. For if everything essential has happened, there is no room for expectation and for hope
(79). It is no longer true that the creation waits with
eager longing for the sons of God to be revealed. For
when an object of hope is seen, that is when the hope
is fulfilled, there is no further need to hope. And in
the end this half-truth becomes as much an opiate as
the purely futurist conception. For the tension is taken
away which makes the Biblical message dynamic and
eventful. By eliminating the most explicit and undeni-
able statements of Jesus and the apostles about the
future coming of the Kingdom and the need for watch-
fulness, or by repeating the old error of the nineteenth-

century modernists that such sayings are merely a
temporal mythological form to express timeless ideas—
in short, by failing to distinguish between the Reign
of Christ and the Reign of God—"realized eschatology" is equally guilty of distorting the proportions of
Biblical eschatology.

The fallacy of both types of eschatology which we
have described is that they think too much in quanti-
tative terms. According to the one we have little and
we expect much. According to the other we have
much and we expect little. But Biblical eschatology
does not think in these categories. It thinks in terms
of hiddenness and revelation. Pastor de Pury has
formulated this very clearly: "Christian hope does not
move from less to more. It does not follow the course
of development or progress. It moves from faith to
sight. It moves from something hidden to something
manifested; from a humble Lord to a glorious Lord;
from what is heard to what will be seen. . . . We are
not separated from eternity by a long road of space
or centuries, but by a veil, which may be torn apart
from one moment to another" (80).

The book of the New Testament in which the full
tension between the "not yet" and the "already"
comes to its climax is the Apocalypse. There is no more
futuristic book. But there is no book, either, in which

the present universal Lordship of Christ is taught more
explicitly. We are confronted with the great events
which are to come. But we are not left in doubt that
the central figure of this cosmic history is the King
of kings and Lord of lords who has already been
enthroned and controls the world situation. At the
very outset he is described as the one who *is* and who
is to come. He *has* already made his people kings and
priests but he *will* manifest his power so that the whole
world will have to acknowledge his victory.

The tension between the present and the future,
between Christ's action in the world today and his
action at the end of history finds clear expression in
the passage concerning the four horsemen. The horseman on the white horse has often been interpreted as
a symbol for a belligerent race. It is interesting to note
that quite independently of one another three modern
scholars have come to the conclusion that the horseman is the King Jesus Christ himself. Using similar
arguments Professor Miskotte (81), Professor Cullmann (82) and Father Féret (83) explain that the
white horse is the same as that which in the nineteenth
chapter (verses 11-13) bears the name: The Word
of God. The victorious horseman is Jesus Christ,
whose word wins in spite of the sharp competition of
the powers of destruction. Of this King it is said, "He

rode conquering and to conquer" (Revelation 6: 2). For he *is* already the powerful King to whom the victory belongs. But the manifestation of his victory will only take place when the race is finished and the other forces have been wholly overcome.

CHAPTER IV

The Kingship of Christ in the Church

The revolutionary change which has taken place in the realm of ecclesiology is based on a very simple discovery—namely, that the King-Messiah and the people of God belong together (84). It is inconceivable that the Christ, the Anointed, who not only announces but represents the Reign of God, should not create a royal people. The messianic expectation of the Old Testament includes the formation of a truly faithful new Israel. The Servant of the Second Isaiah represents at the same time the coming Messiah and the messianic nation. The Son of man of Daniel (Chapter 7) receives a Kingdom which belongs at the same time to "the saints of the Most High."

If we approach the New Testament from this perspective—a perspective which its constant reference
to the Old Covenant forces us to take—it is no longer
an open question whether Jesus has formed a new
community. It is true that he comes in the first place
to claim the allegiance of the whole people of Israel
and that he maintains this claim until the very end
when he dies as King of the Jews. But precisely because
it becomes increasingly clear that Israel will reject
him, he gathers the nucleus of a new people of God.
This becomes manifest in the choice of the twelve
who represent the Israel of the future. It is furthermore implied in the frequent use of the symbols of
the shepherd and the sheep and of the family of God.
Now the sayings about the "ecclesia" are to be understood in this wider context. If Jesus speaks of the
"church" (Matthew 16: 18), he refers to the messianic
community which is, as it were, the new "edition" of
Israel and will accomplish the mission which the old
Israel refuses to accomplish. "Ecclesia" is nothing less
and nothing more than the name of the "assembly"
of God which accepts the King whom God has sent
and thus becomes the true embodiment of the people
of God.

This "ecclesia" Jesus calls "my church" (Matthew
16: 18), just as the sheep are called "my sheep" (John

21:15). The new community belongs to the Christ, to whom the Father has given them. From the outset the Church is a people, who belong with body and soul to their King and whose very existence is bound up with his Kingship.

During the days of the ministry of Jesus the new community represents, however, more a promise than a reality. It has as yet no distinct outline and exists in a provisional manner only. Before it emerges as a distinct entity the great turning point in the history of God must take place. The decision as between the old and the new Israel must be taken. There comes the moment when there is no people of God, or rather when the people of God consist of the only faithful one, who carries all by himself the burden and the promise of the work of salvation. Christ on the Cross *is* the true Israel. One died for all. It would seem that this means the end, but in reality it is a new beginning. The resurrection leads to the formation of a new Israel, which is not an Israel according to the flesh but according to the Pentecostal spirit.

In a sense nothing has changed, for God's work goes on. The new Israel realizes, as James puts it, "God's original concern to secure a People from among the Gentiles to bear his Name" (Acts 15:14). The great promises once given to the nation of Israel are now passed on to the spiritual nation, the Church of God. But in another sense everything has changed (85). This is indeed a new people: new in that they are no longer of one blood and include Gentiles as well as Jews, but new also in that deeper sense, that they belong to the new age, the age of the Kingdom, and that they are—not by sight but by faith—new creatures in Christ.

The new people belongs to the Lord, whom God has set at His right hand. Therefore, the Lord can say to Paul: "I have many people [*laos*] in this city" (Acts 18:10). And Paul speaks of "the churches of Christ" (Romans 16:16). But that is not the whole truth. The Church is not merely an instrument at the disposal of the Lord. The relation is far more intimate and far more comprehensive. This is indicated in two conceptions which express the fundamental theological insights of St. Paul, namely, the formula "in Christ" and the image of "the body of Christ."

In the first Epistle to the Thessalonians Paul speaks of "the churches . . . which are in Judaea in Christ Jesus" (I Thessalonians 2:14; cf. Galatians 1:22). Is this just another way of saying that the Church is the Church which recognizes the Lord? No, it is more. This becomes clear if we compare this verse with such passages as: "If any man be in Christ, he is a new

creature" (II Corinthians 5:17) or "There is therefore now no condemnation to them which are in
Christ Jesus" (Romans 8:1). It is typical that in both
these passages "to be in Christ Jesus" is somehow
linked up with temporal conceptions. It would seem
that Paul refers to a new historical situation. And this
is indeed what he means. Those who are in Christ are
no longer living under the same conditions as they did
before. In the fifth chapter of Romans and the fifth
chapter of II Corinthians Paul develops the conviction
that, just as in and through one man all men have
come under the regime of sin and death, so through
one man all can enter into the newness of life. The
same reality is clearly summarized in I Corinthians
15:22—"as all die in Adam, so shall all be made alive
in Christ."

To be in Christ means then to enter into the new
situation which Christ has created through his death
and resurrection. He is "the beginning, the firstborn
from the dead" (Colossians 1:18). To be in him is
to participate in the new beginning and in the victory
over death. The formula "in Christ" expresses a Christocentric theology of history (86). The death and
resurrection of Christ mean that the whole condition
of man has changed. The event of Jesus' coming is
not a mere event of the past. It is in the literal sense

of the word an event which happened once *for all*. It has made a difference, a difference of cosmic dimensions. To live in the light of and in the strength of that central and decisive event is to enter into a wholly new existence. Those who are in the Church which is "in him" are no longer governed by the old laws, but by new laws which he has exemplified in his life and death.

Now the image of the body speaks of the same reality (87). It is of course true that Paul uses that image to describe the interdependence of the members of the Church. But that interdependence is precisely so indispensable and inevitable because the body is the body *of Christ*. In other words the Church is not merely a body in which the members should render one another assistance as they do in every healthy body. The Church is the concrete, visible manifestation of the crucified and risen Christ in the world. The Church is that aspect or part of Jesus Christ which is tangibly present in the world. That is why the exhortation to fraternal forbearance and collaboration in I Corinthians 12 is dominated by a phrase which runs literally: "For as the body is one, and hath many members, . . . so also Christ" (I Corinthians 12:12). In the Epistle to the Ephesians the concept of the body is used for the sole purpose of making clear that the

Church exists only in Christ. Here the identity of the image of the body and of the formula "in Christ" is most easily recognized. In the passage (Ephesians 2:14-22) concerning the reconciliation of Jews and Gentiles in the Church it is affirmed that this reconciliation takes place "in Christ" and that the new unity thus created is unity in the one body. We may therefore conclude that the Church, according to the teaching of the New Testament, is so related to Christ that he is embodied in it. The risen Lord continues to work in the world and the way in which he is present is in and through the Church. To be "in Christ" or to be a member of the body is to be drawn into the sphere of his action, which is no less than the re-creation of the world.

Now this high doctrine of the Church can easily be misunderstood. Instead of taking it as an indication of a new historical situation we may interpret it as a mystical identification of Christ and the Church. The New Testament guards against this danger first of all by its teaching concerning the *Lordship* of Christ and then again by its emphasis on Christ as the *Head* of the Church. There is no complete mutuality between Christ and the Church. Christ does not depend on the Church in the same way the Church depends on him. The initiative comes from the Head. The growth of

the Body is directed by the Head ("from whom" in
Ephesians 4:16) and it is toward him (verse 15).
There can, therefore, be no question of a direct identification of Christ and the Church. Christ remains
the King and the members of the Church remain the
King's people. "The fulness of Christ" (Ephesians
4:13) is not the present condition but the final goal
of the Church. That Christ is Head of the Church
expresses, therefore, "the eschatological reserve" which
is characteristic of the situation of the Church in the
world (88).

In all that has been said it is implied that the situation of the Church in the history of God is highly
ambivalent. Its very existence speaks at the same time
of an "already" and of a "not yet." It is the people of
God in the great interim period between the coming
of Christ and the coming of the Kingdom. Since so
much depends on the right understanding of this
situation we must try to analyze it somewhat more
fully.

The Church is not only a place where the great
eschatological realities are announced. It is itself an
eschatological fact. The outpouring of the Spirit at
Whitsuntide is a fulfillment of the prophecy concerning "the last days" (Acts 2:17). The Holy Spirit itself

is an earnest (Moffatt: "pledge"—II Corinthians
1:22) of the future and its present activity means, in
the words of Cullmann, "that the final period has
begun, although the old age has not yet disappeared"
(89). Christians can therefore be said to have "tasted
. . . the powers of the world to come" (Hebrews
6:5). This period is the time of the Reign of Christ.
And the Church stands in the center of that Reign.
It is the place where the good news that Christ has
already begun his Reign is known and is proclaimed.
And through that witness in word and deed it belongs
to the new age. It knows the great mystery that one
man has already reached the ultimate goal and that
in him and through him it is possible to participate
in the renewal of humanity and of the world. Karl
Heim says: "In the time between the reconciliation
and the fulfilment there is only one who is in that
condition of fulfilment in which at the end the whole
creation will be. . . . We can have part in that condition of fulfillment, if we become a part of the person
of Christ" (90). Thus the Church has a great deal to
say if it is asked what has happened *already*.

But none of these tremendous realities concerning
the Church are true if they are not seen in connection
with the other side of its life: the side of the "not yet."
The only *raison d'être* and function of the Church is

precisely to be the faithful instrument of God's plan in the period *until* the Lord comes. Its task is therefore a provisional one. The Church is not an aim in itself. Skydsgaard says: "Everything in the Church of Christ is dominated by the 'not yet.' That does not mean that it is not yet reality, but it means that it is still a hidden reality" (91). The Church lives by faith and not by sight. It is a Church of pilgrims who have not yet arrived at their destination or of migrants who have not yet reached their permanent city.

It is, then, highly dangerous to blur the frontier between the Church and the Kingdom of God as happens so often in Roman Catholic ecclesiology. When Karl Adam says, "The Church is the realisation of the Kingdom of God on earth" (92), we can only answer that a Church is to be pitied which does not hope for the manifestation of something more and better than its own life. When Congar speaks of the Church as "the extension of the life of God . . . God's life itself . . . the divine society itself" (93) and when Vonier calls the Church "so perfect, so definitive as the glorified Christ is in his perfection, that is in his final victory" (94), we can only consider such statements as anticipations which weaken rather than strengthen the Church. For a Church which does not know that the Kingdom is its promise and its vis-à-vis becomes a Church in monologue. It is so at one with its Lord that it confuses its own voice with the voice of the Lord. It is so much at home in what it conceives to be the Kingdom that it no longer expects the Kingdom. No, the Church serves the Kingdom. It lives by the "dynamis" which the Kingdom has brought into the world. But it is not the Kingdom. It is, in the words of Emil Brunner, "an essentially imperfect society. . . . The Church transcends itself. . . . It can only be understood from the end. To be in the Church is to be oriented toward the final goal. . . . The Church can therefore not be an end in itself; it aims at that which comes afterwards, the Kingdom of God, of which it is only the earthly, historical, hidden aspect in the form of a servant" (95).

In this perspective it becomes very clear why it is a matter of life and death for the Church to understand the true meaning of Christ's Kingship. The "already" reminds us that Christ is reigning here and now. But the "not yet" reminds us that this Kingship is a priestly and prophetic Kingship. We know the King only by faith; we do not see his glory and may not act as if we were already transplanted in the glorious Kingdom. The Church is a Church of sinners who need at all times to be reconciled to God by the priestly Christ and to be nourished by the word of the prophetic Christ. The King reigns but he reigns from the Cross and through the Word.

What does this mean for the life of the Church? It means first that it must at all times and in all things be in living contact with the King. The Church exists only in permanent dialogue with its Lord. Whenever and wherever it refuses or forgets to listen to him and to answer him, to be judged by him and to be renewed by him, it becomes just a human, all too human association for the maintenance of spiritual ideas and moral standards. That is the great tragedy of all churches which identify their own life with the life of Christ or which know Christ only as a religious teacher. They renounce the greatest of all privileges of the Church, which is to be constantly re-called, re-formed and re-created. They get finally imprisoned in their own systems and, whatever may be their human productivity, they become sterile from the point of view of God's work in the world.

But even the church which proclaims clearly that Christ is its King and that therefore nothing, not even the traditions of the church itself, may come in between the Lord and his people is constantly in danger of saying "Lord, Lord" without actually following him. For the church lives in a world in which all the old powers still operate. And since it is inclined to overestimate its own achievements, convinced as it is that it is always dealing with the affairs of the Lord, it becomes an easy prey for the tempter who suggests that it can live by its own force. Clericalism is not merely the sin of hierarchs who take their own power too seriously. It is the sin of every church which is more interested in its own life than in the service of the Lord. Reformed or unreformed, *all* churches are in constant danger of declaring with the Church of Laodicea that they are rich, that they are well off, that they lack nothing, when in fact this very declaration shows them up as pitiful, poor, blind, naked churches who lack everything because they are no longer in direct touch with their King. It is a strange and terrible thing that so many churches who affirm the faith that there is no other justification than by faith alone take, in their synods and assemblies, in their propaganda and reports, precisely that tone which St. Paul calls "glorying" or "boasting" and which is in fact the ego-centric self-assertion of the church. There is perhaps no surer sign of the sickness of most of our churches than this naïve affirmation of their own excellency and achievements. And there is no clearer proof of the fact that all reformation is instantaneously threatened by deformation.

"*Ecclesia reformanda, quia reformata*" ("The Church is to be reformed, because it is reformed") is therefore a truth that cannot be taken too literally. For "reformation" is an event, not a status. It is a gift which loses its meaning when the immediate contact with the Giver is broken off. For a church which has been reformed it is, therefore, a sin against the Holy Spirit to consider its reformation as an inherent quality of its own life rather than as a "charisma" which it must receive every day and for which it must pray constantly. One of the most adequate descriptions of the Church is that of Pascal: "*Bel état de l'Eglise quand elle n'est plus soutenue que de Dieu*" (The Church is in good condition when it is supported by God alone"). The first public pronouncement of the King of the Church was: "Repent ye." And the first public word of the Reformation was Luther's first Wittenberg thesis: "Our Lord and Master Jesus Christ desires that the whole life of the faithful should be a life of repentance." But the tragedy of the Reformation churches is that this explosive truth, which was destined to give birth to a constantly re-formed church in daily renewed communication with Christ, was considered as an achievement and a ground for glorying. Thus the churches of dynamic repentance became churches of arrested repentance. They took refuge in

their dogmatic systems or in their spiritual and moral
traditions. They dug themselves in, instead of remain-
ing on the move. They fought battles for sterile victories. For they did not realize the critical and exclusive meaning of the "triumph in God through our
Lord Jesus Christ" (Romans 5:11) which implies
triumph in troubles and weakness rather than in
strength.

That is why the proclamation of the Kingship of
Christ in the Church is a matter of life and death for
the Church. Where the King is not proclaimed or is
proclaimed only in a pious but irrelevant manner, the
Church loses its birthright. It becomes the lonely
Church, the Church in monologue, the sick Church
which does not realize its own sickness. But where the
Kingship is actually recognized, where in sober realism
and radical self-criticism the Church dares to face the
judgment of the Lord, there the Church discovers the
true measure of his grace and is born again through
his creative action.

These are not theoretical truths. For this is precisely
what we have seen in recent years in several of the
European churches. As the Kingship of Christ was
rediscovered with its full radical significance, there
came upon many in the churches a keen realization
of the sickness of the Church. Could it truthfully be

maintained that these profoundly secularized church bodies with their immobility, their self-satisfaction, their lack of faith and courage were the people of the King of kings? Could the Church demand that the world should acknowledge the King if it did not itself show fruits of repentance and obedience? It was in and through the battle which it had to fight that the Church came to see more and more clearly that it needed radical reformation. And the course of the battle reaffirmed that insight. It became manifest that the Church was even more undermined than it knew. Large numbers of those who had been considered faithful Christians went over to the enemy or refused to prove their professed allegiance to Jesus Christ. Theologians and church leaders were not lacking who thought up profound reasons for a profitable compromise with paganism. But precisely the nearer the Church came to the point where it had no other helper than its Lord, the greater became its certainly and the clarity of its message.

But once again the Church had to be reminded how little it can count on itself and how easily it falls from reformation into deformation. The renewal of the Church had hardly begun when the forces of conservatism and reaction began again to assert themselves. Parties and man-made traditions were not ready to abdicate. Must we then take it that it is only in a moment of fright and under the pressure of the enemy that the churches are willing to take their King seriously? Has the judgment of recent years—which like all judgments was in the first place addressed to the Church—left the Church quite unshaken? Has the tragedy taken place which Dr. Kraemer described in the beginning of the war in the words: "There is nothing more dreadful than to imagine a Church emerging from this period without an inner change"? At the moment we cannot answer these questions, for we are in the midst of a situation in which reformation and deformation, a concrete recognition of the royal right of the King and the desire to return to the status quo are in conflict. But it is quite clear that if the new insight into the Kingship of Christ is not translated into the realities of church life, it will again fade from the consciousness of the Church and the Church will once more deny its greatest privilege.

What happens when a church takes the Kingship of Christ seriously? We can here only try to indicate some of the most important characteristics of such a living church.

Now the first one is surely that it proclaims clearly what the Christian faith is and what it means con-

cretely for us today. We have seen that according to
the New Testament the specific function of the
Church is no other than to render witness to its King.
We have also seen that that witness is "kerygma," the
announcing of decisive events in the relations between
God and man, God and the world. The church which
knows itself to be the instrument used by the King for
the salvation of man speaks, therefore, without uncertainty and confusion about the victory of its Lord and
the relevance of that victory for the life of man today.
That is the meaning of that much used and abused
expression: a confessing church.

A confessing church speaks under constraint. It says
those things concerning its Lord about which it cannot be silent unless it is to deny its own *raison d'être*.
It passes on what it has heard as the Lord has made
the word of Scripture come alive. It overcomes constantly the confusion of tongues which arises so easily
in its own midst, by desperate attempts to bring men
of diverse insights together before their Lord, so that
they may listen together and speak together. It cannot
possibly accept the Church's neutralizing its own message by speaking through mutually contradictory or
mutually exclusive voices.

And it speaks concretely. Whether it means business or not will become clear in the degree of precise-
ness of its message. A confessing church proclaims the

full implications of the acceptance of Christ as King. It calls the practical denials of the Lord in the life of church and society by their true name. And it does not do so only when the church is directly attacked, but equally when the church is seemingly respected and when its plain speaking will mean a considerable loss of popularity and prestige.

There comes a moment in the life of a confessing church when it must clearly formulate its faith. Whether that moment has arrived or not depends most often on the situation with which the church is confronted. When grave spiritual dangers threaten its life from within or from without the time has come to speak very explicitly, to commit the whole church, to nail it down in such a way that there is no room left for uncertainty or ambiguity. That is how most of the classical confessions came into being. That is what the churches were again forced to do during the church conflicts of recent years.

But what is the place of such formulated confessions? They are the signposts which the church puts up to indicate the way along which it is led by its Lord, as it pursues its pilgrimage in the world. Signposts—serious warnings as to what is the true and what is the false road. But only signposts—not to be confused with the place to which they point.

A confessing church is, therefore, something funda-

mentally different from a confessionalist church. In
the latter the formulated confession is considered as
an ultimate criterion. One cannot get around it. It
stands between the church and its Lord as he speaks
in the Scriptures. As a Dutch theologian has put it:
"A church which ascribes absolute authority to its
confessions, and devotes its energy to their conserva-
tion is a confession-church. A church which recognises
the relative authority of the confession and recognises
together with the confession the absolute authority
of the Scriptures is a confessing Church" (96). Or as
Dr. Kraemer puts it: "The possession and functioning
of a confession does not make a church a confessing
church in the sense of the New Testament, but the
action of concretely confessing (Christ) with the risk
of suffering for his name's sake" (97).

The confessions retain their very great significance
as answers which the Church has given, as decisions
which it has taken in its attempt to obey its Lord. We
shall never be able to confess clearly and truly unless
we pay serious attention to their affirmations and negations. But when all is said and done we must give the
answer for our generation and take the decisions demanded here and now. Hans Asmussen puts it clearly
when he says that the confessing church owes its existence to the insight "that the true doctrine must hap-

pen" (98) and that, therefore, it must be proclaimed with new words and in relation to present-day issues.

The Church confronts specific challenges in each period of its life. It cannot answer those challenges by a reference to its decisions in bygone ages. Just as the creeds of the early Church do not contain a direct answer to the crucial problems of the sixteenth century, so the Reformation confessions do not answer the vital questions which had to be answered in recent years in Germany, in Norway, in Holland and elsewhere. And none of the old confessions go far enough in that witness which is specifically entrusted to us, namely, the witness to the Kingship of Christ and against all false lords.

It follows that a church which takes the Kingship of Christ seriously is a church in which preaching is speech on behalf of the King. Whether a church is on the way to renewal or not depends on its sense of responsibility for the representative message which is uttered in its name from its pulpits. Does the church accept preaching that degenerates into lecturing about religious experiences, moral advice, spiritual hygiene, social or international problems? Or does it not rest content until its preachers know that their mandate is to announce the great deeds of God in Christ as witnessed to in the Scriptures? Here again the lesson of the years of struggle is important. For at that time it became very clear that the church can take a stand and maintain it only where it is built on the rock of the words that will not pass away. From all fronts of the battle of those years there came the unanimous testimony: God's Word comes alive; God's Word happens; it and it alone gathers the church. And so in these various churches there was a turning away from the sidetracks to the royal road. But the great question is again whether this will last. Will many consciously or unconsciously think that the uncompromising and incisive sermon based on the radical, hard and strong statements of the Bible is all right for times of trouble, but that we may just as well return to more easily digestible subjects in time of peace? Or will the Word of God overcome our dullness of peacetime as it overcame our fear in time of war?

A church which takes the Kingship of Christ seriously is furthermore a church which reflects in its life the universality and cohesion of the people of God and the body of Christ. Now the tragic result of the secularizing process during the last centuries is that instead of manifesting those characteristics and so giving shape to the social process the churches have become themselves the prey of secular social forces. In their daily life they appear to be influenced by the inexorable laws of sociology rather than by the creative force of the Holy Spirit.

Thus the churches have ceased to represent the unity of all classes, races and nations in Christ. They are no longer able to manifest that the Lord gathers men and women who are separated by social barriers. Because of the lack of understanding which they have shown for the problems of the more dynamic and creative classes of society—the labor class and the intelligentsia—they have become more and more identified with the middle class. In their social, moral and cultural judgments they give the impression of interpreting the bourgeois spirit rather than the Spirit of Christ. Thus the danger arises that the ties which bind the church members together become a strange mixture of Christian convictions with unconscious assumptions and prejudices which are rooted in middle-class mores rather than in the Gospel.

For the same reason the congregations do not exemplify clearly what true Christian fellowship means. The forces which have played upon their life are strongly individualistic in character. It is not difficult to discover how deeply even the most orthodox churches have been influenced by an atomistic conception of society and how that conception has under-

mined the true Biblical notion of common membership in the one body. The result is that many
congregations have degenerated until they consist of
unrelated individuals who attend church services for
private reasons.

In the quieter days these realities about the life of
the Church were largely hidden beneath the surface
of old traditions and pretensions. But in the years of
conflict the true situation was clearly revealed. Congregations which were just the public of a pastor
proved completely unable to meet the test; congregations which were held together by the bourgeois spirit
were largely wiped out when the anti-bourgeois storm
arose. But at that critical moment it also became manifest that even today the Lord gathers the Church. For
new communion was created as men and women—
not infrequently from outside the Church—took a
common stand for Christ.

It is the shock caused by the failure of the Church
and the gratitude for the gift of new fellowship in
Christ which has led to the realization that in this
respect also the Church must repent and show fruits
of repentance. The congregations must confront the
small proportions of their life with the proportions of
the Church Universal in which they pretend to believe;
they must face the judgment pronounced upon them

by the King who desires his Church to be a sign of
the unity and universality of his Kingdom; they must
therefore let themselves be mobilized for his service,
make a desperate attempt to break out of their soci-
ological imprisonment and go out to those classes of
men from which they have become separated. At the
present moment the realities of Church life are a
denial of the message that Christ is King. We may
not rest until that offense—which is not the offense
of Christ but of men—is removed.

Finally a church which takes the Kingship of Christ
seriously is one which seeks to restore the unity of the
Church of Christ. If there is only one King, if salvation means to be part of the one Body, no church
can accept the fact that the people of God are scat-
tered and that the Body is broken. It is not for the
sake of greater efficiency in its practical tasks, not for
the sake of a common front against common enemies,
it is for the sake of keeping faith with the King, whose
Kingdom cannot be divided against itself, that the
churches must enter upon the difficult pilgrimage
toward visible and tangible unity.

But precisely because the only unity which is in line
with the specific mission of the Church is unity in
Christ, the search for unity can never be separated

from the obedient following of his will. In other words unity can never be an aim itself. Christian unity is only found as churches turn together to their common Lord. As Professor van Niftrik puts it: "The search for the unity of the Church must be identical with the search for Jesus Christ as Head and Lord of the Church" (99). And true unity can, therefore, never be bought at the expense of that truth which is manifested in Christ himself.

The churches are on the way toward the recognition of their membership in the Church Universal. Here again the war years have unexpectedly borne fruit. Precisely when ecumenical relationships became invisible, the churches discovered the price of their sharing in the world-wide fellowship. And much of this has remained alive in the postwar period. We need only compare the nature of interchurch relationships today with that of the twenties to see that in this respect also something has happened to the churches. The essential oneness of the Church of Christ is no longer a vague and distant ideal, but a reality which operates in the life of the churches.

The grave question remains, however, whether the churches have understood the full implications of a truly Christ-centered unity. Do they realize that once they have started on this road there is no going back?

Do they see that they must now be ready to follow the Lord of the Church along uncharted roads? Have they discovered that ecumenical fellowship is not a matter of general friendliness and tolerance but a matter of struggling with each other for the true knowledge of and obedience to Christ? Are they willing to let themselves be called to order by their fellow churches in the name of the common Lord? And are they willing to accept responsibility for the life of the other members in the Body?

Unless these questions find positive answers, the ecumenical movement will get stuck before it is really under way. For the very nature of that movement demands that it shall proceed to these deeper regions. What is at stake is the reality of the Church of Christ in this world. We can, therefore, not be satisfied with correct relationships between the churches and inter-church collaboration in matters of common interest. These things can only be the introduction to the tackling of the real issue, which is the manifestation of the Una Sancta, one in faith and sacrament and holy in its unreserved consecration to the Lord.

We have reason to be grateful for the remarkable expressions of Christian solidarity which the churches have given in different realms, but the final test comes in the realm of an even deeper solidarity where

churches prove their willingness to learn and to receive
what the Spirit says to and through their sister churches
and where they manifest their concern for the truth
and purity of the life of these sister churches. In other
words, the reality of the ecumenical movement depends on the service which it renders to the renewal
of the Church. The ecumenical question is simply
another aspect of the crucial issue which all churches
have to face but which they are called to face *together*:
Will they or will they not repent of their unfaithful-
ness and turn again in absolute confidence to their
Lord and King in order to be made anew? The *Una
Sancta* comes where churches are united in seeking
to become the Una *Sancta*.

CHAPTER V

The Kingship of Christ in the World

We have already seen that the affirmation of Christ's Lordship over the world is no less central in the New Testament message than the witness of his Lordship over the Church. The King of the Church is the King of the world. We must now try to define more clearly in how far these two forms of sovereignty are similar and in how far they are different.

It is a striking fact that many of the statements which the New Testament authors make about the world correspond exactly to those which they make about the Church. This is already implicit in the Gospel of Matthew, which seeks to demonstrate that

Christ is the true King of Israel and which closes with the proclamation that to him all power in heaven and on earth have been given. According to the Johannine writings Christ has come to save those which God has given him: He is the good Shepherd who lays down his life for *his* sheep; but he is also the Lamb which takes away the sins of the *world* and he is the Saviour of the *world*. The two affirmations that he is the propitiation for *our* sins, that is, for the sins of the faithful, and also for those of the *world* are brought together in I John 2:2. Similarly St. Paul can speak in one and the same passage of the reconciliation as Christ's ministry to "us," that is, to the *Church* (II Corinthians 5:18), and also as Christ's work for the *world* (verse 19).

The most explicit statements concerning the relatedness of Church and world in their common dependence on the Lordship of Christ are to be found in the Epistles to the Ephesians and to the Colossians. Here Christ is not only the Head of the Church but also the Head of the whole creation. Both Church and world exist in him and through him. And the two are brought into the closest relationship. Christ has been set "as head over everything for the church, . . . which is his Body" (Ephesians 1:22-23). "He is the head of the Body, that is, of the church" and as such he has "pre-eminence over all," that is over the whole world (Colossians 1: 18).

What does this convergence and interrelation of the statements about the Church and the world mean? It means that the history of salvation, of which the Church is the main instrument, embraces far more than just the life of the Church. That history deals not only with the fate of individual souls and the destiny of the people of God. God thinks and plans in terms of humanity and of the universe (100). The fact of Christ is, therefore, not only the decisive fact for those who recognize its true significance. It is the center of *all* history. It changes the situation of the whole world. Individuals and communities, Jews and Gentiles, all have to confront the same crisis and to decide for or against their true Lord. The Church has a very specific function to perform in this critical period. It is the pioneer, the advance guard of the Kingdom of God. But this shows precisely that it is not an aim in itself and that it is to serve the world.

Church and world have, therefore, a great deal in common. Both have the same Lord. Both live in the light of the same victory of Christ over the powers of sin and death. Professor Cullmann has expressed this situation in the image of two concentric circles of which Christ forms the center (101). The Church is the inner circle, the world the outer circle, but both together are the realm over which Christ is King.

But how can we square these extremely positive statements about the world with that other aspect of the New Testament message which we find precisely in the same authors and according to which the world is the realm of Satan, the symbol of all that Christians must renounce and the merely provisional framework of life which is to pass away? How can God love the world which we are told to flee? How can it be reconciled to Him and still be destined to perdition?

We must not expect to receive an absolutely clear and logical answer to these questions. For the New Testament authors do not reason in the manner of observers who try to define the essence of things in logical categories. They proclaim divine events; they speak as participants in the drama of salvation and they conceive all things in the light of the changing perspectives of that drama.

Thus they can look at the world from two different angles. The world is on the one hand God's creation which remains the object of His purpose of salvation in Christ. But it is on the other hand that part of humanity which has confirmed its enmity against God by rejecting His Son. The New Testament can, therefore, speak of the *kosmos* as the whole of reality which

God embraces in His will to save. But it can also speak of *this* world, the present age, as the world which has not received the light. This dialectical passing from one view of the world to another is inherent in the eschatological situation in which the Church finds itself. The *crisis* has come in Jesus Christ. He has come to claim the world; "he came to what was his own" (John 1:11). But the world did not recognize him. The crisis becomes, therefore, a judgment. "Now is this world to be judged; *now* shall the Prince of this world be expelled" (John 12:31).

But this "now" is only true in Christ, who represents the Kingdom of God on earth. It is not yet true in a visible manner. The full manifestation of the judgment is yet to come. What we *see* is the continuation of the old world. God's answer to the rebellion of that world is to make Christ King over the world and to begin the creation of a new world. The Church is the realm where the King is acknowledged and where the new creation is already taking place. It is the realm where the two ages overlap: "this age," which is in reality the passing age, and the "coming age," which is invisible but actively present through the Holy Spirit in the Church.

It is, therefore, inevitable that the word "*kosmos*" should be used in two different connotations. It is

used in a positive manner in order to show that God's
plan remains a "cosmic" plan. He does not give up
His universal purpose and does not narrow His aim,
though He pursues it in a different manner as He prepares the way for a wholly new world. But the same
word is also used in a negative sense to indicate the
world which has signed its own death warrant by rejecting its true Lord.

Does this mean that the Church is only concerned
with the *new* world and that it should leave the *old*
world to its fate? It is clear that those who belong to
the sphere of the new creation must not let themselves
be captured by the antiquated world. The Church is,
therefore, to be fundamentally independent of the
world; it is not to live according to the laws which
dominate the life of secular communities, but has its
own specific laws. But that does not mean that the
Church is indifferent about the life of the present
world. It remembers that its Lord rules already outside
as well as inside the Church and that he uses the
worldly powers for his purposes. It remembers, moreover, that in spite of its rebellion and in spite of the
judgment which it has brought upon itself, this world
is the world which God created, to which He sent His
only Son and which He has never ceased to love. And
while the Church does not know how much of the

old creation will find its place in the new creation, it hopes that God will use whatever elements in it may be found worthy of re-creation. The Church seeks, therefore, to force the world to declare its true intentions. The world must face the question whether it owes allegiance to the Prince of this world or to the King of kings. The *kosmos* which accepts reconciliation with God must be disentangled from the *kosmos* which remains in revolt against its true ruler. The territories which have been occupied by the usurper must be claimed in the name of their legitimate Lord.

In this war there can be no truce and no peace, for the powers of this world remain feverishly active and never capitulate willingly or finally until the day of the manifestation of Christ's victory. The situation of the world remains ambiguous until the end of time. The *kosmos* is by definition a battlefield. But while the battle continues to rage, there can be no doubt about its ultimate outcome.

The Gospel is, therefore, equally far away from a Manichaean dualism which rejects the world *in toto* and from an optimistic faith in the gradual penetration of the world by divine forces. In fact, the New Testament does not theorize about the world; it demands decisions with regard to the world. It demands that we let ourselves be liberated from the domination by the world and that we represent in this world the Kingdom of Christ.

It is in this light that we can grasp the real difference between the Church and the world. That difference is not that the one belongs to Christ and the other is left to itself. Both belong to him, but the Church knows the King, while the world does not. In the Church his Kingship is revealed; in the world it is hidden. The Church lives as the people who know that the victory *has* been won. The world lives on as if nothing had happened. The Church realizes that the powers which militate against God's plan are under control. The world lives on as if these powers were still able to shape the ultimate destiny of men.

But this is not all. The Church not only knows about the victory; it shares in the victory. It is the realm in which the new creation is already taking place. It is "in Christ," that is to say, it belongs to the new age of which he is the pioneer. The present world does not belong to that age. It also will be re-newed but that will be at the end of time, when a new heaven and a new earth will replace the present world. It is already in "crisis" that is, under judgment, but it does not realize its perilous condition. Now the world cannot find out by itself what is its true situa-tion. It must be confronted by the fact of Christ. The

Church, which is consciously and willingly under the
Head, must share its knowledge with the world, which
is unconsciously and unwillingly under the same Head.
The Church, which is that part of creation in which
Christ's actual Kingship is already acknowledged, owes
to the rest of creation the announcement that this
Kingship concerns all men and all powers.

But at this point we must face a perplexing question.
Is the difference between the Church and the world
as clear cut as we have made it appear? Is there not a
third possibility? Can there not be civilizations or
nations or institutions which recognize the Kingship
of Christ and so cease to be "world" in the sense in
which we have just used that term?

It is true that the peculiar difficulty and complexity
of the relation between Church and world in our
Western world comes precisely from the fact that we
live in a so-called Christianized world and in half-
secularized churches, so that the sharp distinctions of
the New Testament seem somehow inapplicable to
our condition. But the basic situation has not changed.
Wherever the Church becomes again the voice and
manifestation of the new age the frontier between
Church and world becomes only too evident. And
how thoroughly and easily the "Christian West" can
fall back into pure and unadulterated pagan worldli-

ness has been demonstrated with terrible clarity in our day and generation.

Is the proclamation of the Kingship of Christ then a merely quixotic undertaking? What is the use of reminding the world of Christ's Lordship if we cannot expect a true response? Our answer must be that, even though the Church has no illusions about the nature of the world, it owes to the world the witness concerning its true Master and Lord. While it does not expect any permanent or total victory until the full manifestation of the victory of Christ, it must implement its faith in his present Kingship by constant battle with the forces of the enemy. The reality of its faith is at stake. In this battle it seeks to keep in check "the dethroned powers which still rule the world." Even though these powers will never admit that they have been overcome, they may recognize that they are not alone in this world and that they must reckon with the power of the King. There is an important and relevant difference between worldly powers which know no other law than the law of self-assertion and mutual destruction and powers which recognize, however dimly, that they are confronted by an authority which transcends their own life. No nation or civilization has ever lived in willing obedience to its true King, but there have been nations or civilizations which have realized that there is a King whose commandments cannot be transgressed with impunity.

The Church preaches, therefore, the message of the King not only to individuals but also to communities, states, nations. According to Ephesians 3:10 the mystery which was hidden in God, namely, that His cosmic design finds full expression in Jesus Christ, must be made known by the Church to the powers of this world. The Church does not have a Christocentric individual gospel and a social gospel consisting of moral advice. Its one message, that Christ is Lord of all, is to be proclaimed to all. There is a difference between its message to individuals and that to society. But this lies at another point.

In preaching the Lordship of Christ to individuals it offers them the opportunity of becoming new creatures in Christ. In demanding that society recognize the Lord it offers the promise that through following his commandments it shall be saved from self-destruction by the demonic powers in its own midst and live in justice and peace.

The Old Testament describes the task of the prophet as that of a watchman. In Ezekiel the Lord says to the prophet: "I have made thee a watchman unto the house of Israel. . . . Give them warning from me" (Ezekiel 3:17 and 33:7). Similarly the Lord says according to Isaiah: "I have set watchmen upon thy walls, . . . which shall never hold their peace day nor night" (Isaiah 62:6). From the days when Ambrosius warned the Emperor Theodosius until the days when the Church of Norway protested against the crimes of National Socialism the Church has based itself on those texts, when it found itself constrained to render a prophetic warning to the world. Now the watchman's role is to announce events. The Church as watchman warns the terrestrial city that the King has come to take charge of the city and that all will have to render account to him.

In carrying out that office the Church must be mindful of its privileged situation. In its relations with the world it need not have an inferiority complex. It has received knowledge of the real situation in which the world finds itself without realizing it. It may live out of a wonderful certainty, while the world remains in utter uncertainty. It knows the true history of the world which is, in the words of Barth, "the secret reality of all history, since it is history itself" (102). But if this is really so, the Church has no reason to speak apologetically or to adapt the content of its message to the categories of the world. It has no right to withhold the one message which it is decisive for the world to know and which is the very *raison d'être* of the Church's mission to the world. The Church is not to speak *against* the world, as if it considered the world its enemy. It is precisely characteristic of the situation that, whatever the world may do to the Church, however it may make war upon the saints, the Church cannot forget that the world *has* been overcome, that its destiny *has* been decided and that, therefore, its denials and negations cannot change the ultimate outcome. The Church must, therefore, not fight back when it is attacked by the world. It should rather answer all opposition and all persecution by an even more joyous and certain affirmation that in spite of all its Lord reigns. This is the only way in which it can show the world that it means what it preaches.

If the Church lives up to the proportions of the message with which it is entrusted it will show no signs of anxiety or fear in its relations with the world. After all, the world is not half as dangerous for the Church as the Church is for itself. The mortal danger for the Church is that it should cease to be the Church, not that it should be oppressed from the outside.

At this point we must remind ourselves again of the priestly and prophetic nature of the Kingship. For it is precisely in relation to the world that the Kingship can easily be isolated and has been isolated from its true context. The Church proclaims Christ's Kingship over the world as a *priestly* Kingship. The Church's witness·to the world must, therefore, be rooted in intercession. There are times when that is practically the only ministry which the Church can render. But in such times it realizes that this ministry is no less powerful than the direct witness. The Church represents the priest who has borne the sins of the world. It is to follow him in this complete solidarity with the world and to pray for forgiveness of the sins of nations, states and indeed humanity. But it begins by confessing its own sins. If it does so, it will be saved from Phariseeism and moralism and its witness to the world will be all the more convincing. For just as self-justification by one calls forth self-justification by others, so the simple word of repentance is met by an echo of repentance.

The Church will also express its priestly nature in accepting that its way to victory, like that of its Lord, is the way of the Cross. The Revelation of St. John describes the Church as companionship "in tribulation, and in the kingdom and patience of Jesus Christ" (Revelation 1:9) and shows thus that the Kingship is in this world conditioned by the acceptance of the Cross. The Church knows that it can live in that situation with gratitude and joy.

The Church proclaims Christ's Kingship as a *prophetic* Kingship. It will, therefore, not attempt to make the Kingship directly visible in the world. In the present dispensation in which "we see not yet all things put under him" (Hebrews 2:8) Christ rules through his word. At the time of the temptation in the desert his only defense is the divine word. And during his whole life this remains his only weapon. The glorious King described in the Book of Revelation is armed with a sword, but, as we can learn from the prophets, this sword is the sword of the Word of God (103). His victories are spiritual victories. The Church has no right to claim any other power or to use any other means of persuasion than those which its Lord has used. It is in the impossible position of claiming the whole world for a King who does not allow it to use any of the instruments by which the claims of kings in this world can be backed up in order to be respected. But the Church knows that the sword of the Spirit is in the long run more powerful than any other sword.

The Church must, therefore, distinguish very clearly between the Kingship of Christ and the domination of the Church over the world. The Kingship means Christocracy but not ecclesiocracy. The Church is called to speak in the name of its Lord. But if it does so, it remembers precisely that it does not speak in

its own name and that there remains the distinction
between the body and the head, between the instrument of the royal government and that government
itself. It is on this point that we must reluctantly part
company with our Roman Catholic brethren. The
encyclical "*Quas Primas*" of 1925 concerning the
institution of the feast of Christ the King gives in its
beginning an admirably clear definition of the Kingship of Christ and of its Biblical basis. It emphasizes
strongly the universal character of Christ's Reign. But
—almost in passing—it suddenly declares that the
Church *is* precisely this Kingdom of Christ which is
destined to cover the whole earth. Thus the demarca-
tion line is blurred. Christocracy becomes in fact
ecclesiocracy. The Church becomes an aim in itself.
The consequences of this attitude become visible in
the later sections of the encyclical. We find there a
protest against the fact that the Church is not allowed
to legislate for and govern men in view of their eternal
salvation and against the fact that the Roman Catholic
Church is "shamefully" put on the same level with
other denominations. Thus the very real danger of
the identification of the Church and its Lord is made
manifest. A Church which does not observe the
eschatological reserve automatically transforms the
priestly and prophetic Kingship into church-centered

power politics. Its own existence and prosperity become more decisive criteria than the will of the King himself.

This confusion between theocracy and ecclesiocracy, which has found its strongest expression in the claims of the medieval popes, became the main reason for Luther's anti-theocratic reaction and his emphasis on the separateness of the two realms. In the Calvinistic Reformation theocracy came again into its own, but the confusing element of secular methods to achieve spiritual ends crept in once more. This explains the violence of the denial of theocracy in the name of tolerance and freedom which characterized the progressive forces of the eighteenth and nineteenth centuries. The very idea of Christ's Kingship over the world seemed a medieval superstition. The Church had no business with the life of state or society.

But this reaction, which has not yet spent its force, is based on a false alternative. The choice is not between ecclesiastical power politics on the one hand and the withdrawal of the Church from the world on the other. *Tertium datur.* Theocracy, or rather Christocracy, does not necessarily mean that the Church attempts to force its convictions upon the state and the nation. Its true meaning is that the Church announces what it believes to be the word of Christ for the world, but that it does not use any other means of persuasion than the truth of its message. In other words there is a Christocracy which uses exclusively the prophetic means of the word and the priestly means of prayer and leaves it to the King himself to make these means effective.

In his remarkable critical analysis of the theories of Church and state in the early Church Dr. Berkhof comes to this conclusion: "The Church must again dare to preach the theocratic commandment. But it must do this in such a way that it does not exclude, but include tolerance" (104). That is not only the lesson of history; it is the conclusion to which we are forced by a serious consideration of the royal office in the context of the threefold office of Christ. Christ desires to be obeyed for his own sake and not because of ulterior motives. In his relations with men he refused systematically to use the worldly and demonic means. He demanded free and willing obedience. The Church which represents such a King can do no more and no less than to pass on his word and must have absolute confidence that that seemingly defenseless and power-less word will act as a two-edged sword.

It might seem that in all that I have said about the Church and the world I have already dealt with the problem of the state. But the state is not merely an aspect of the world. It has a peculiar function and dignity. The very fact that we use such terms as "Kingship," "Lordship," "Reign" points to the existence of a relationship between the history of salvation and the realm of secular government. We must try to define that relationship more precisely.

The question of the theological foundation of the state is one of the burning issues in present-day Continental theology. Is the state to be considered in the light of the general order of providence, of natural theology, of common grace or has it a place in the order of salvation and is it to be understood Christocentrically? The problem is by no means academic, since it has a very practical bearing on the attitude which the Church or individual Christians take to the state. In fact it is so relevant to political decisions that its discussion easily takes on the aspect of a political rather than a theological debate. And it cuts across all confessional differences as the Thomist doctrine of natural law, the Lutheran doctrine of the two realms and the Calvinist doctrine of common grace are equally called in question. I will not attempt to give a full analysis of the debate (105) up to date, but will state briefly why I believe that the Christocentric conception of the state is true.

In the light of the doctrine of the Kingship of Christ it is a priori to be expected that the state stands under the Lordship of Christ. *All* power has been given to him. The New Testament does not know a general providence apart from the history of salvation. The reconciliation concerns the whole world. But there is also much specific evidence that the state is actually seen in the light of Christ's work of salvation.

Recent exegetical studies have shown that the Biblical authors consider the state as the organ of superhuman forces, forces which are in themselves neither good nor bad, which may serve the plan of God but which may also, if they run wild, turn against God. The "authorities," the "principalities" and "lordships" which play such a great role in New Testament thought find their expression and manifestation on this earth in the power of the rulers. That is why the main word which characterizes the state, "exousia" or "authority" means not only governmental power but also cosmic force.

This notion is perhaps not as strange as it appears at first sight. Have we not all learned something about the existence of "isms" and "utopias," of "myths" and "ideologies" which take hold of the life of states and nations and which, if they are not kept in check, become truly demonic?

Now the New Testament teaches that these powers are subject to Jesus Christ. As I Peter 3:22 has it, the fact that he sits at the right hand of God means that the authorities and powers have been submitted to him. Whether the rulers are aware of it or not, they perform a function within the Reign of Christ. That is why the most explicit passage which we have about the state, Romans 13, is set in a context in which the members of the Body of Christ are urged to reflect in their life the universal love which God has shown in Christ and to overcome evil by doing good. They do not need to revenge themselves for (to use the words of Karl Barth): "evil men are in fact controlled by the order which God, the Father of Jesus Christ, has set up in the world outside of the church, since Christ is the King and Lord over all powers and rules powerfully" (106). The rulers are intended to be the servants of God and of His ultimately gracious purpose. St. Paul uses a very telling expression when he calls them even the "liturgists" in the service of God. They have to use the sword, but they must use it for the benefit of men and for the sake of justice. In the provisional order which exists during the Reign of Christ the state has the *positive* function to make life on earth possible and it is, therefore, in spite of its forbidding appearance, an instrument of God's mercy.

Now the "authorities" which manifest themselves in the life of the state may openly or in a hidden way revolt against their true Lord. For although Christ reigns truly and all cosmic powers have been subjected to him, they have still a considerable freedom of movement. They can no longer win the ultimate victory but they can still achieve shadow victories. If that happens, the state is no longer the servant; it becomes the Beast which makes war upon the saints. That is why the New Testament can pass from a very positive to a very negative view of the state.

What are the consequences of this Christocentric conception of the state for the Church? It is clear that a Church which knows that its Lord is the Lord of the state cannot accept a fundamental dualism between the spiritual and the political realm or a complete separation between the Christian life in the sphere of the Church and the Christian life in the sphere of the state. A Church which believes in the actual Kingship of Christ will, therefore, protest against any and every attempt of the state to conceive politics as an autonomous realm or to absolutize its own life. Such a Church will remember that its task is, as De Quervain puts it, "to understand the state better than it understands itself" (107). And it will demonstrate this by rendering a positive prophetic witness to the state, not only when the state is in danger of denying its true mission but also when it needs the support and guidance of the Church in order to fulfill that mission. The Church intercedes for the state and it does so in the hope which is expressed in the prayer of intercession of the Dutch Church: "that government may be so directed that the King of Kings may rule over both rulers and subjects."

The doctrine of the present Kingship of Christ over the world provides the basis for a social gospel which is truly a gospel. We do not need to choose between an individualistic pietism which forgets the cosmic proportions of the Biblical message and a social moralism which neglects its eschatological character. We do not need to choose between an exclusively priestly witness which announces only the forgiveness of sins and has no place for the law of God and an exclusively prophetic witness which preaches the law but does not offer the gift of grace. We have a priestly and prophetic King. We do not need to crown him, for he has been crowned with glory (Hebrews 2:7,9). And because he reigns already we may and must see the world and all that is in it as the theater on which that glory is to be manifested. This is a great liberation. We are freed from the narrowness of introspective religion and set

in the stream of God's world-embracing plan. We are
also freed from the despair engendered by the impotence of our moral idealism. The question of success
becomes secondary. We do not need to be assured
that the Gospel "works." The one all-important thing
is to be with the King and to obey him. The issue is
not whether we will succeed in establishing his Kingdom; the question is whether we live right now as his
grateful subjects expecting that what is already given
us "in spe" ("in hope"), will come to us "in re" ("in
fact"). Such an eschatology is not an opiate. It is a
call to active service.

It is often taken for granted that the only possible
basis for Christian action in the realm of state and
society is some form of natural theology. Thus Arch-
bishop Temple said at the Malvern Conference that
the great choice to be made is: "Do we or do we not
follow the Reformers in their rejection of all natural
theology?" He added that the decision against natural
theology leads straight to the complete separation of
the spheres of Church and state, for in that case the
Church is concerned wholly and solely with the work
of grace and it has no right to approve or disapprove
the action of the state (108). But with all due respect
to Archibishop Temple's theological insight we must
say that this is a false alternative. It is possible to take

one's stand on the Bible alone and to arrive at social and political ethics which have a critical and constructive bearing on the life of the state and society. In fact, if we let the Bible have its say and listen also to the things in it which are hard to hear for modern ears, it forces us to see everything in the world in the perspective of divine events which have their repercussions in every sphere of life.

The question may, however, be raised whether this also applies to the *content* of the social ethic. Even if it is true that the foundation of the social ethic is apparent in the Biblical message, must we not admit that its content must be sought in the natural law?

I do not believe that we are forced to this conclusion. On the contrary. If at this point we open the door to natural theology, all that we have said about the Kingship of Christ has been in vain. For it is precisely the tragedy of all natural theology that it introduces a rival king who tends to assume more and more authority. This becomes very clear in Thomist theology. Sertillanges states very frankly that we must "place faith and reason on two thrones, not equally high but recognising the sovereign rights of each" (109). Our answer must be that this leads to a serious limitation of the sovereignty of Christ, for the enthronement of reason means the enthronement of man, who becomes his own lawgiver. But there is more. Natural law is necessarily the law of the old Adam and of the present age. A social ethic which is based on the insights written in the hearts of men lacks the eschatological perspective which is distinctive of the Christian ethic. It ties the Church to the world instead of liberating it. It tends to comfortable compromises instead of dynamic witness. St. Thomas says: "*Lex nova super veterem addere non debuit circa exteriora agenda* (110). In other words: in external matters, in society and state the coming of Christ and his victory have made no difference. But that amounts to denying that Christ's present Kingship has any bearing on our life in the world.

Does the Bible then contain all things necessary for the Christian life in the world? It does, in the sense that it gives us the basic insights concerning God's design for man, for society, for the state which we need to arrive at Christian decisions in these realms. That does not mean that the Bible presents us with ready-made recipes. The picking and choosing of single texts and the literal application of such texts is a denial of the unity and historicity of the revelation. If I isolate a Bible text from the whole, I act as master rather than as servant of God's Word. And if I copy the actions of Biblical persons, I deny that God's

Word is a living Word, which reaches me here and now. The danger of Biblicism in its various forms is that the specific historical situations in the Bible are absolutized and become a wall between God and ourselves instead of a window through which we see God's work among men. There can, therefore, be no question of the *direct* use of the laws which have been given for the social and political order of Israel. The Church as the new Israel is not bound to any nation; and no nation, however Christian it may appear to be, can claim to be the successor of the old Israel.

In which sense can we then speak of the sufficiency of the Bible as a foundation for the social ethic? The Biblical witness as a whole with its proclamation of the great deeds of God and of the commandments of God given to Israel and to the Church is the great signpost which shows us the direction in which we have to go, if we are to serve the King. The Bible does not give a ready-made answer to the question, What is God's Will for us today? But it does show us what road the army of the King has traveled and where it is going. Or to change the image: The Bible gives us the general map of the region in which we have to operate as soldiers of the King. But we do not know the precise place where he will use us at any given moment, unless he marks that spot himself on the map. That is why a Biblical social ethic has no place for casuistry. But also why it has a place for serious study and reflection. We need all the help of our faculties of imagination, reason and observation in order to understand the structure, the inner cohesion and purposefulness of God's design for ourselves and for the world and in order to find our own definite place in that plan.

It is strange that after these many centuries of Church history we have to admit that in this respect the Bible is still very largely a closed book. We have only the vaguest ideas about its message concerning the abiding realities of social and political life. We operate with a few obvious texts or a few general principles, but we know next to nothing about the Biblical witness with regard to such basic elements of our common life as property, justice, work, soil, money. Now on these matters the Bible has a great deal to say. In all these respects it would save us from our deep-rooted paganism. But we have become so accustomed to think that for our conception of property we should turn to jurists inspired by Roman law and that for our conception of other economic factors we should turn to the textbooks inspired by capitalistic or Marxist materialism that we do not even discover the gulf between our thought and that of the Bible. And most of our books on Christian ethics do not help us, because they also take it for granted that Christian ethics are the elaboration of some isolated, so-called Christian principles rather than a serious reflection on and conversation with the Biblical witness.

Just as we need a Biblical theology, so we need a Biblical social ethics. Once again that does not mean the uncritical and naïve imitation of situations which are not our own. But it does mean to take seriously what has been revealed to Israel and to the Church. It would be folly to seek to force the remarkable social laws of Deuteronomy upon our modern nations. But it is by no means foolish to ask what lies behind these laws, what conception of man, of his relations to his neighbor and to God's creation, how all this is fulfilled in Christ and how it may guide us in our understanding of what obedience to the Lord means today in our society. At this point the thorough historical study of the Bible is not an enemy but an ally of Biblical theology and ethics, for it helps us to discover the true meaning of the Biblical conceptions, to enter much more deeply into the strange, rich world of the Bible and to distinguish much more clearly between the rough stuff of Israelitic or Hellenistic life and its transformation in the hands of God.

The social, or better, cosmic gospel must base itself

on the Bible as a whole, on the gospel of the Old and
New Testaments and on the law that forms part of
that gospel. Every truth about God has its social and
political implications. Every dogma has its ethical consequences. A social gospel worthy of its name is therefore not an additional gospel, but simply the pro-
longation of the Gospel itself. In a recent study (111)
Karl Barth has introduced the concept of parable or
analogy to make clear what bearing the truths by
which the Church lives have on the life of the secular
community. The actions and decisions of the Church
in the secular realm seek to express by analogy what
the Church is and what it confesses. The incarnation
finds its analogy in concern with individual men;
justification in concern with justice; the liberty of
God's children in civil liberty; the ecumenical character of the Church in international understanding.
I believe that this is indeed the way along which the
Church should advance. For it is the royal way, the
way of the King. The Church whose Lord is Lord of
the world need not look elsewhere for its marching
orders. All that it needs is to turn to its King and to
receive again and again his priestly gift of himself and
his prophetic word. The great question is whether it
has sufficient faith to count on him alone and not to
divide its allegiance. If it has, it will find that it is

never left without the knowledge of his will and the power to do it.

The task of the Church in the world is to shout in the streets of the city: "Blessed be the King that cometh in the name of the Lord; peace in heaven and glory in the highest." It will of course be rebuked for this message by some of the Pharisees. But it will have to answer: "If we will hold our peace, the stones would immediately cry out."

The following notes refer to books, many of which will not be easily available in North America. They are, however, given in order to show what materials have been used as a basis of the author's survey of recent European theology. They should also serve the purpose of acquainting readers in North America with authors most of whose names have perhaps not yet become sufficiently well known on their side of the Atlantic.

1. In this Calvin was inspired by Bucer.
2. *Institutio* II:15:1.
3. See Dr. J. Koopmans in *Het Ambt van Christus*, 1942, p. 24.
4. See Heidegger in Heppe, *Reformierte Dogmatik*, 1935, p. 365.
5. Matthew 28:18.
6. Colossians 2:15.
7. Ephesians 1:22.
8. John Amos Comenius, *The Bequest of the Unity of Brethren*, English edition, Chicago, 1940.
9. Luther says in his *Preface* of 1522 that in the Book of Revelation "*Christus weder gelehrt noch erkannt wird*" ("Christ is neither taught nor recognized"). In the *Preface* of 1530 his judgment is more positive.
10. Karl Barth, *Kirchliche Dogmatik* II:1:712.

11. Harald Diem, *Luthers Lehre von den zwei Reichen*, Munich, 1938, pp. 107 ff. Cf. A. de Quervain, *Kirche, Volk, Staat*, Zurich, 1945, pp. 203 ff.

12. *Der Staat und der Mensch*, Stockholm, 1946, p. 365.

13. Hanns Lilje, *Luther*, Nuremberg, 1946, p. 199.

14. Commentary in Mark 16:19. Cf. commentary in Matthew 28:18 and I Corinthians 15:27.

15. Cf. Wilhelm Niesel, *Die Theologie Calvins*, Munich, 1938, p. 220.

16. *Institutio* II:15.

17. *Institutio* IV:20:1.

18. Thus *Institutio* IV:20:16. Cf. Barth, *Der Staat als theologisches Problem*, 1939, pp. 31-32.

19. Dedication of I Timothy; letters to Edward Seymour, Edward VI and Sigismund August of Poland.

20. *Op. cit.*, p. 220. Cf. de Quervain, *op. cit.*, pp. 206 ff.

21. Quoted in Ragaz, *Der kampf um das Reich Gottes*, p. 234. Cf. Miskotte, *Hoofdsom der Historie*, Nijkerk, 1945, p. 417.

22. Heppe, *op. cit.*, pp. 362, 384, 386.

23. *Der Christliche Glaube*, 1828, pp. 259-260.

24. *Ibid.*, pp. 262, 263.

25. Renan, *Vie de Jésus*, edition Nelson (first edition in 1863), p. 10.

26. *Ibid.*, pp. 88-89.

27. Paul Wernle, *Jesus*, 1916, pp. 269, 271.

28. Renan, *op. cit.*, pp. 186, 187. "Ne méprisons pas cependant cette chimère, qui a été l'écorce grossière de la bulbe sacrée dont nous vivons."

29. Harnack, *Wesen des Christentums*, pp. 27-28.
30. Quoted by Holmström, *Eschatologisches Denken der Gegenwart*, p. 44.
31. Troeltsch, *Gesammelte Schriften* II:522.
32. *Ibid.*, p. 848.
33. Troeltsch, *Glaubenslehre*, p. 36.
34. *Religion in Geschichti und Gegenwart* (first edition), "Aemter Christi."
35. *Begegnungen*, Wuppertal-Barmen, 1936, p. 3.
36. *Von der Nachfolge Christi*, Berlin, 1923, pp. 11, 8, 9.
37. See *Römerbrief*, 3rd edition, p. 91.
38. *Auferstehung der Toten*, p. 59.
39. *Der Mittler*, Tübingen, 1927.
40. *Kirchliche Dogmatik* II:1:714 ff.
41. *The Student World*, Second Quarter, 1932.
42. It was thus understood by Berdiaev, *Orient und Occident*, 1929, p. 1.
43. *Die Lehre vom Wortes Gottes*, 1932, I:1:160-161.
44. *Zeugnisse der Bekennenden Kirche*, Tübingen, 1946, vol. I, p. 62.
45. *Die Kirche Jesu Christi*, 1933, p. 8.
46. *Theologische Existenz Heute*, 1933, p. 11.
47. *Ansbacher Ratschlag* of 1934.
48. *Evang. Kirche in Deutschland und Judenfrage*, p. 143.
49. *Zeugnisse*, p. 37.
50. *Ibid.*, p. 70.
51. *Ibid.*, p. 88.
52. *Kirchliche Dogmatik* I:2:55.

53. *"Die Kirche und die politische Frage von heute,"* 1938, reprinted in *Eine Schweizer Stimme,* Zurich, 1945.

54. *Kirchliche Dogmatik* II:1:715-719.

55. *Der Staat und der Mensch,* Stockholm, 1946, p. 336.

56. *Ibid.,* p. 379.

57. Paul Althaus, quoted by Einar Molland in a remarkable article in *Norsk Teologisk Tidskrift,* 1946, p. 3, which analyzes the theological implications of the Church conflict in Norway.

58. *Promemoria* of the theological faculties, 1942.

59. *The Struggle of the Dutch Church,* American edition, pp. 83, 86.

60. *Ibid.,* p. 29.

61. *Ibid.,* p. 32.

62. *Ibid.,* p. 60.

63. *Spandauer Synode,* July, 1945, p. 12.

64. Pierre Charles, S.J., *La Robe sans Couture,* Museum Lessianum, p. 118.

65. Jean Daniélou, S.J., *Protestantisme Français,* Paris, 1945, p. 436.

66. *Les Premières Confessions de Foi chrétiennes,* Paris, 1943.

67. *Ibid.,* p. 48.

68. See Stauffer, *Die Theologie des Neuen Testamentes,* Geneva, 1945, Anmerkung 360.

69. Cf. Colossians 1:16; 2:10.

70. W. G. Kümmel, *Verheissung und Erfüllung,* Basel, 1945, in which the whole recent discussion concerning the Kingdom of God is clearly summarized.

71. Schniewind, *Das Evangelium nach Matthäus*, Göttingen, 1937, p. 136.

72. Kümmel, *op. cit.*, p. 95.

73. Other examples in K. L. Schmidt's article, "Basileia," in Kittel's *Dictionary*.

74. Except I Timothy 6:15.

75. Cullmann, *La Royauté du Christ et l'Eglise dans le Nouvean Testament*, Paris, 1941; *Christus und die Zeit*, Zurich, 1946.

76. According to Grundmann this is the "*Urchristologie*," which lies behind all further Christological thought. See Kittel's *Dictionary*, vol. III, p. 404.

77. See Kittel's *Dictionary*, vol. I, p. 453.

78. In an essay, "*Le mystère du Fils de l'Homme*," to be published in the near future.

79. "*Cessons de rien attendre d'essentiel de l'avenir*"— Féret, *L'Apocalypse*, Paris, 1943, p. 141.

80. Roland de Pury, *Présence de l'Eternité*, Neuchâtel, 1943, pp. 176-177.

81. Miskotte, *Hoofdsom der Historie*, Nijkerk, 1945, p. 137.

82. Cullmann, *Christus und die Zeit*, Zurich, 1946, p. 142.

83. Féret, *op. cit.*, p. 148.

84. K. L. Schmidt in Kittel's *Dictionary*, vol. III, p. 525. Braun. *Aspects nouveaux du problème de l'Eglise*, Fribourg, 1942, p. 105.

85. Franz Leenhardt, *Etudes sur l'Eglise dans le Nouvean Testament*, Geneva, 1940, p. 18.

86. Stauffer, *Die Theologie des Neuen Testamentes*,

Geneva, 1945, p. 275. Cf. Stauffer in Kittel's Dictionary, vol. II, p. 437.

87. Karl Heim, *Jesus der Weltvollender*, Berlin, 1939, p. 264, Cf. Bonhoeffer, *Nachfolge*, Munich, 1940, p. 162.

88. Schlier in Kittel's *Dictionary*, vol. III, p. 680.

89. Cullmann in *Evangelisches Missionsmagazin*, July, 1941, p. 100.

90. Karl Heim, *op. cit.*, p. 262.

91. Skydsgaard, *Godsrijk en Kerk. Onder Eigen Vaandel*, April, 1939, p. 129.

92. *Das Wesen des Katholizismus*, p. 26.

93. Congar, *Chrétiens Désunis*, Paris, 1937, p. 59.

94. Quoted by Grosche, *Pilgernde Kirche*, Freiburg, 1938, p. 70. Grosche himself, who is also Roman Catholic, gives a much more Biblical answer.

95. Emil Brunner, *Das Gebot und die Ordnungen*, Tübingen, 1932, pp. 511-512.

96. T. Dokter in the *Weekly* of the Netherlands Reformed Church, February 15, 1947.

97. *De Roeping der Kerk*, The Hague, 1945, p. 66.

98. Asmussen, *Kirche Augsburgischer Konfession*, Munich, 1934, p. 31.

99. Dr. G. C. van Niftrik, *Kleine Dogmatiek*, Nijkerk, 1944, p. 185.

100. The Church is only a part, though the central part, of the Reign of Christ.

101. *Christus und die Zeit*, p. 166.

102. *La Confession de l'Eglise*, Neuchâtel, 1934, p. 53.

103. See Féret, *L'Apocalypse*, pp. 123 ff.

104. H. Berkhof, *De Kerk en de Keizer*, Amsterdam, 1946, p. 164.

105. Cullmann gives such an analysis in *Christus und die Zeit*, pp. 169 ff.

106. *Kirchliche Dogmatik* II:2:806.

107. Alfred de Quervain, *Kirche, Volk, Staat*, Zurich, 1945, p. 202.

108. *Malvern*, London, New York, Toronto, 1941, pp. 12-13.

109. A. D. Sertillanges, *Saint Thomas d'Aquin*, Paris, 1931, p. 55.

110. Quoted in Troeltsch, *Soziallehren*, Tübingen, 1919, p. 274.

111. *Christengemeinde und Bürgergemeinde*, Zurich, 1946, p. 247.